uMama

RECOLLECTIONS OF
SOUTH AFRICAN MOTHERS
AND GRANDMOTHERS

COMPILED AND EDITED BY MARION KEIM

SUN MEDIA

Umama - Recollections of South African Mothers and Grandmothers

Published by AFRICAN SUN MeDIA under the SUN MeDIA imprint.

First edition 2009, first printing 2009
Second printing 2009
Second edition 2017, first printing 2017

ISBN 978-1-928314-32-5
ISBN 978-1-928314-33-2 (e-book)
DOI: 10.18820/9781928314332

Set in Palatino and Univers

Cover design by Sally Swart.
Cover image of Nelson Mandela's mother by Alf Khumalo.
Design and layout by mr design.

SUN MeDIA is an imprint of AFRICAN SUN MeDIA. Academic and prescribed works are published under this imprint in print and electronic format. This publication may be ordered directly from www.sun-e-shop.co.za.

Produced by AFRICAN SUN MeDIA.

www.africansunmedia.co.za
africansunmedia.snapplify.com (e-books)
www.sun-e-shop.co.za

CONTENTS

DEDICATION

This book is dedicated to our daughters Thandi and Joy and all the children of South Africa in the hope that as they grow up they will see, feel, share and reciprocate the endless love of their mothers and grandmothers.

For their sake I long for a South Africa of peace, love and care, where children can grow up safely, where mothers do not have to shed tears in sorrow, pain and fear for their children, where women are respected and honoured for their roles in their families, communities and society and for their contribution to our humanness.

INTRODUCTION

When I gave birth to our daughter Thandi and became a mother for the first time, I was overcome with an indescribable, deep and limitless sense of love and joy. In the weeks that followed, fears and challenges about my own role in her life began to occupy my mind. What will I be able to provide for my daughter? What will she need from me? What can I do so that she will become all that she can be? And most important of all, how can I ensure that she will become a compassionate and loving human being?

Looking for answers, I remembered my own mother and the uncon-ditional and selfless love she surrounded me with while I was growing up. Only in my later years did I become aware of what she had sacrificed for me in her young life. I remembered the story of her mother – my grandmother – and how she had held her daughter – my mother – over her head during the Second World War, up to a window of a train loaded with soldiers passing our village on their way to the front lines of battle. One of these soldiers was her husband, my grandfather, who could just catch a glimpse of the two-week-old girl he had yet to meet. Despite being left on her own with two small children, my grandmother helped many others in her small village, Neckarzimmern, giving extra care to the prisoners of war housed in the village in the hopes that her husband's Soviet captors were treating him equally well. But her husband never returned. He was declared 'missing in action', leaving my grandmother at age thirty-one with two children to support and raise, and with ques-tions that would never be answered about her husband's final days.

My grandmother played a central role in my upbringing, looking after me and my cousins while my parents were working. I remember the day after her death at age eighty-seven when we found letters from the International Red Cross addressed to her, dated as recently as two years before her death, indicating that she had never given up the search for her husband.

I left Germany for South Africa only months after Nelson Mandela's release in 1990. Having lived more than half my adult life in South Africa, I have come to know countless mothers and grandmothers who have moved me with their dedication, their endless patience and their unstop-pable ability to love and nurture despite their own difficult circumstances and the trials of history that remain upon their shoulders and in their hearts.

These women, these mothers and grandmothers of South Africa, have for many years been my teachers. They have taught me what I would not necessarily have learnt elsewhere.

Collectively these women are an important part of what gave birth to the new South Africa. Yet their lives and their contributions have gone unrecorded.

I have gathered these stories of the South African women represented in this book because I wanted to capture what South Africa's remarkable mothers and grandmothers have given to me, because I wanted to honour what they have contributed to my own becoming, because I wanted more people to learn what I have learnt, and because I wanted my own daughters to be moved in ways that I have been moved – moved toward what is good, what is strong, what is caring and what is just.

In compiling this book I asked South African women and men from different backgrounds and different walks of life to write a story about their mother or grandmother, a story they want to tell and to share with the public of what their mother or grandmother meant to them, what insights and values she passed on, what stayed with them because of her. Some found it easy to write, others did not; some agreed enthusiastically, others struggled and took a bit longer but still came forward with the most amazing stories. The intention of this book is not to create any laureates or odes; rather, the book should be seen as a collection of stories which speak to all of us directly in our wonderful multicultural society about a universal phenomenon – our mothers and grandmothers and what they mean for us today.

This book is for mothers and grandmothers throughout the world, women who continually sow but often are unable to reap; who give but do not always receive; and who pray but are often not prayed for. And this book is for us, their children.

As the world changes and our human existence becomes more com-plex by the day, I hope the stories that follow will give us comfort and guidance. I hope as well that they will continue to remind us of who we are.

Marion Keim
September 2017
Cape Town

Kathy Ackerman-Robins & Suzanne Ackerman-Berman

THE GROUNDBREAKER

Wendy Ackerman (née Marcus), born 17 December in Cape Town

As the daughter of a second-generation South African, and the grand-daughter of one of the founders of the first Jewish community in Stellenbosch, our mother has prided herself in integrating the traditional values inherited over generations into her daily life. Because of the historical discrimination against Judaism coupled with the racial discrimination they witnessed in their lives, our parents have taught us never to discriminate in any shape or form. This value has filtered through all aspects of our lives and has become a family legacy.

With this heritage in mind, 'where mom came from' has been an integral part of the role she has played in the building of an ethical company in an unethical society. Our mother's involvement in supporting our dad in building a non-discriminatory company in apartheid South Africa has set the foundations not only for us as children, but for all who have benefited from her passionate belief in youth development, education, the arts, environmental issues and the empowerment of all.

In the early days we remember clearly her passionate attempts at building homes for the staff of Pick n Pay who had no other opportunities available to them. We also remember the endless nights discussing the lack of education opportunities and facilities available to the largest sector of South African society – *she fought the system*. Proof of her struggle is evident today in the success of the many individuals who have benefited from her Educational Foundation and who are today practising as doctors, professors, Supreme Court judges and various artists performing internationally.

She became a groundbreaker in many areas. One that we remember in particular is her identification of the looming crisis as she sat with a family friend, an early AIDS sufferer who had been abandoned by his family. These experiences all contributed to her involvement in the forward-thinking policies on HIV/AIDS at Pick n Pay in the early years.

Suzanne:

My earliest memory of Mom is of her sitting on the floor reading to us every night or playing her guitar in front of the fire. Today, she can be found in her sanctuary, her garden or on the floor at home with her youngest grandchildren or in local schools, trying to make children read or learning to play the latest games with them. As a working mother she had an incredible gift for finding a balance in her professional and personal life whilst pursuing her broad interests. In this way she has become a role model for the working mom. During many challenging times her family has always come first. For me, particularly, she stepped in during my divorce and also became a surrogate mom to my girls when I was hospitalised for six months during a difficult pregnancy.

Kathy:

I remember her taking me to the concerts on a Thursday night from the tender age of eight and, when we were teenagers, exposing us to cultural beauties and museums in small snippets to make us hungry for more. Mom's early passion for the arts runs in her veins. When she was growing up, her father constantly played early scratchy Caruso records. This early exposure worked because today Mom is a passionate supporter and benefactor of the Cape Town Opera and the Cape Philharmonic Orchestra. Mom in turn went on to influence the life choices I have made by becoming an active participant in community development and the arts. Whenever I need her, nothing can keep her away! Mom's patience with helping me through my challenging moments at school and through university has taught me to be a patient and involved mom.

Mom is an endless source of information, particularly when she quotes from literature, poetry, music and her great speciality, Shakespeare. Her grandchildren are constantly tapping into this resource.

She has a wicked sense of humour; her ability to speak her mind and her *joie de vivre* has landed her in trouble so many times! She has the gift of the gab, not only in the boardroom but also round the dinner table.

She has incredible personal style, always immaculately turned out, and her granddaughters are already reaping the benefits of that.

As a wife, I believe that after fifty-one years of marriage she can teach us all a thing or two about love, tolerance, patience and survival! She has supported Dad in all areas of life and through many difficult and challenging times. They have always faced adversity together, with a sense of humour, a sense of what is right and a clear vision.

As a mom, she had been supportive and kept up with the latest fashion and music trends of the time, thereby staying involved and creating an open and welcoming home to all our friends. She has always been a tolerant mom. Yet, when a boyfriend and I broke curfew, she was on the doorstep brandishing punishment in her pyjamas!

As a grandmother, she brings a smile to the faces of all her grandchildren, from ages six to twenty-one. She has always had an amazing ability to cross the generation gap and, therefore, she and her grandchildren keep each other entertained for hours. She has been seen on all continents with grandchildren trying to keep up with her hectic educational tour.

The amazing thing about Mom is that she has the ability to identify the interests and talents of anyone close to her and she will ensure that she is as interested and knowledgeable about the topic at hand, whether it be *Star Wars*, wrestling, magic, rugby, fashion, music, technology or the challenges of teenage life today!

Suzanne & Kathy:
Mom, you have really had a profound impact on all our lives and your legacy of giving, teaching and appreciating the beauty of life in its many forms will carry on through generations. 'Shall I compare thee to a summer's day? Thou art more lovely and more temperate' – William Shakespeare, Sonnet 18.

Kathy Ackerman-Robins and **Suzanne Ackerman-Berman** grew up in Cape Town and currently lead a number of initiatives for the Ackerman family. Suzanne is the Transformation Director of the Pick n Pay Group and Kathy heads up the philanthropic foundation of the Ackerman Family Trust.

Kader Asmal

THE ANCHOR OF MY CHILDHOOD

Rasool Asmal (née Maithir), born in the first
decade of the twentieth century in Stanger,
died 25 December 1968 in Stanger

I was the sixth of eight children born to Ahmed and Rasool Asmal. We
lived and grew up in a 'company' town, servicing the sugar-cane industry
on the north coast of old Natal.

My mother was born in Stanger at the beginning of the twentieth
century just before the Bambata Rebellion of 1906 and died on Christmas
day, 1968. A customary marriage arranged when she was in her teens,
to a dashing and happy-go-lucky immigrant from India, put a heavy
burden of family-rearing on her shoulders not helped by the early diag-
nosis of diabetes.

Her diabetes caused her to suffer much of the time of my childhood,
but this did not affect her infinite capacity to rear us. In a male-dominated
and heavily patriarchal society, mothers were usually relegated to the
background, but in our case my mother was the anchor who provided
stability and guidance in our lives.

Growing up during the War was a harsh experience for many because
of rationing and other shortages. My mother ensured that there was
food on the table, shirts on our backs and shoes polished for school. We
lived in overcrowded homes, with little privacy and with outside lava-
tories. No motor car and no holidays. But there was no disgruntlement
among us, no overweening demands for 'better' things in a society
where wealth was the index of status.

I don't think my mother ever went to school, simply because it was
inconceivable early in the century for a Muslim girl to do so. In any event,
there was no school she could have attended. Yet, she ran a household of
ten adults virtually single-handedly, especially after my father became a
migrant shop assistant following the collapse of his little fruit and ice-
cream shop.

She instilled in us the absolute need to live within our means, which has meant that none of us later became big capitalists! Some sacrifices had to be made, and it was painful for all of us, and especially for her, that the brightest of the Asmals, the second-born, had to leave school at the end of primary school in order to augment the meagre family income.

My mother was illiterate in the precise sense of the word. But her inability to read and write did not preclude her deep feelings for education, which she nurtured among the male children. Ours was a close-knit family and she encouraged those who had to leave school early and were at work to assist those who were at school or who wished to enter higher education. She didn't understand our homework, but she insisted that we did it. We were too poor to give *zakaat*, the tithe that those who could afford it had to pay, but my mother's approach was one of solidarity rather than charity.

In the claustrophobic society of the fifties, with police informers and the passage of savage laws by the apartheid regime, it would have been easy to have retreated into a selfish private world. But this was the period of my political education. My mother raised no objection to my political awakening when I supported the boycott of schools (as a schoolteacher!) and brought the iconic Albert Luthuli, president of the African National Congress, to my home, an unheard-of experience for most 'Indian' families. All my mother wanted was that I should explain what I was doing. Too many books, she used to tease me, too many ideas, for a small head!

Small-town politics and narrow parochialism passed her by. She lived for her family but did not entirely subscribe to the sentiment that 'every beetle is a gazelle in the eyes of a mother'; she could be critical of wrong turns and misbehaviour.

There were many pressures exerted on her to conform to the mores of a small country town. She defended all of us against the outrageous pressures and the sly hints of narrow-minded bigots. I recall one such incident when some neighbours complained to her that I was setting a bad example, as I was too obsessed with books, listened to 'western' music and did not show the appropriate degree of religious piety. I was a 'moffie', they implied – a terrible insult at the time. I recall my mother's anger at what she considered to be the abuse of her son.

If she chastised us for our behaviour, it was with words, never with her hand. In a society where corporal punishment was de rigueur in schools, prisons and homes, this discipline exercised by her set a remarkable example for me – a life-long opposition to corporal punishment. I made a small salute in her direction when I successfully defended the abolition of such violence against children before the Constitutional Court during my tenure as minister of education.

Ours was a very boisterous family, with arguments, debate and loud conversations among the siblings, in a traditional society where silence before elders was considered to be the only form of respect.

Not once did our mother show the slightest inclination to silence us. We loved her because of her tolerance, her gentleness and understanding, values which were not entirely common currency among our relatives in Stanger.

She had little to laugh about, what with the demands made on her, an absent husband and two married sons under the same roof. She made time for all of us and attended to our needs. In my case, she had to respond to my constant and debilitating attacks of asthma from the age of three onwards. Why asthmatics required special treatment is not quite clear to me now but I was not one to oppose the special care and attention I received from my mother. In particular, she used to laugh at the solution she proposed at my not being able to fast during Ramadan because of my asthma. I was appointed official taster of the food for the family and I had to do so standing up in the pantry in the dark to ensure that I did not enjoy this breach of one of the five pillars of Islam.

I have always been curious about the provenance of first names. She would not, though, answer my question about the origin or the meaning of her name. I now realise that it was exceptional to call a woman Rasool. It means, variously, messenger, emissary, envoy, delegate, apostle – all attributes of the representative of the deity. I think she would have smiled wryly if I had told her, with my usual impertinence, that these were qualities associated with the masculine gender.

Finally, her love overcame the anguish she felt when my marriage in 1961 and my political activities precluded my return to my home from overseas. My brothers did not inform her of my marriage to Louise, because one or two of them disapproved of it. Many months later, when she learnt about it, she did not consult her sons but sent the only piece of jewellery she owned – her ring – to Louise. We value it as a memento of a remarkable woman who was progressive in a deeply conservative society and magnanimous when there was so much racial and personal meanness around.

I would like to believe that I inherited from her what Yeats called the 'golden top of care'.

Kader Asmal (1934–2011) was born and raised in KwaDukuza (Stanger) in KwaZulu-Natal. He was a former minister of education (1999–2004) and minister of water affairs in the Mandela government (1994–1999) and member of Parliament in the National Assembly (1994–2007). He was an advocate of the High Court and a professor of Law at the University of the Western Cape.

André Brink

LOVE WILL OUTLAST US

Aletta Wilhelmina Wolmarans, 'Lettie'
(centre), born 16 October 1907 in
Bedford

Almost thirty years after my mother retired it regularly happened on my trips through the country that strangers would come up to me to enquire about her; and in response to my evident surprise they would mention, as if it were the most obvious explanation in the world, that she had taught them English at Boys' High in Potchefstroom. Some would specifically refer to *Three Men on a Boat*, or Thomas Hardy, or *Burchell's Travels*, but most often they would mention Shakespeare. This would invariably be followed by something like, 'You know, it was Mrs Brink who first taught me to love Shakespeare. And I can assure you, it's not just any-which-way kind of love. It's love with a real passion.' And then my interlocutor – teacher, hard-nosed businessman, lawyer, farmer, priest, bank manager or clergyman – would break into quoting, 'Tomorrow, and tomorrow, and tomorrow …', or 'If music be the food of love, play on …', or 'The quality of mercy is not strain'd …', or 'If but this too, too solid flesh would melt …'

I know from my own school years how the course and content of my life were changed by a small handful of teachers – Miss Mostert and Mr Rousseau in Douglas, Mr Van der Reyden and Mr Vlotman in Lydenburg – and how the wisdom they taught me (for their teaching always transcended mere knowledge into the realm of wisdom) will remain with me till my dying day. And so it is with deep understanding and joy that I acknowledge in the many strangers who accost me that special exhilaration of discovery my mother brought to generations of schoolboys. Under her guidance they overcame the clamour of sport, and hormones, and the thousand natural shocks that flesh is heir to, and listened to the voice of the Bard and found their lives changed forever.

She never thought of becoming anything but a teacher. But when she got married she had to bow to the convention that determined the lives of women in her generation to place her family first. This meant that for about twenty years her dreams of teaching had to be kept on the back burner until my youngest brother, Johan, went to school and she could return to her career. Even then, she arranged to teach the early standards in primary school in order to keep an eye on Johan; only gradually did she move through the ranks with him, until she allowed herself to arrive where she had always wanted to be.

During all the years of waiting she'd tried to combat the frustration by doing charity work and devoting herself to women's organisations where over the years she won every available cup and prize for baking, cooking, decorating, needlework and whatever else was on offer. We benefited, of course. Her meals were legendary. But our most lasting prize was to see her happy and fulfilled as the teacher of Shakespeare.

Aletta Wilhelmina Wolmarans, known as Lettie to all her friends, was born on 16 October 1907 in the small village of Bedford. And although her family was as dyed-in-the-wool Afrikaans as my father, whom she met while he was – briefly – at the agricultural college of Elsenburg before he joined the Department of Justice and became a magistrate, her Eastern Cape connection ensured a lifelong appreciation of the English heritage. This meant that even though we were always sur-rounded by staunch Nationalists, my father a Broederbonder till the day of his death, she brought a somewhat more liberal understanding to the world, which helped me to be accepted by the family with a tad more tolerance as a person and a writer. Even though she did threaten at one stage that I would be disinherited if I ever got involved with a girl from Smuts's United Party, when as a student I actually fell in love with the lovely Esther from a 'Sap' family, my mother was the one who went to plead my case. And later, when my books fell victim to censorship and I was vilified by the Afrikaner establishment, and even my father found it hard to deal with an aberrant son, it was my mother who held the family together and made sure that there was always something to appreciate and enjoy together. Politics, and arguments, and fashions, and mindsets, she seemed to know deep within herself, might come and go: what really mattered lay deeper and could not be touched by the mere coming and going of people. In the end, love would outlast us. And beauty. And caring.

And something to laugh about. Mother's sense of humour could be delicate, and subtle, and finely tuned, and impish. But when the occasion demanded, it could also be large and spontaneous and uncluttered and crude. Always a person of emotion rather than cold logic, she was responsible for spectacular explosions of temper in our home. But these thunderstorms were usually over as quickly as they came up, and then her uninhibited laughter would break through the clouds again. Even during her final bedridden years when there seemed to be little to laugh about, she had a bright smile ready for any nurse or visitor in the frail-care centre where she spent her last years. I remember being told by the matron how, one morning, when it was tea time in her ward, the nurse on duty found herself next to my mother's bed, her back turned so that she could minister to the patient in the next bed. Mother leaned over, pulled back the elastic of the nurse's slacks, and emptied her teacup on the poor woman's backside. Thank heavens, the tea was no longer very hot.

For years, her main desire was to die so that she could be with my father again. But it took almost fifteen years of waiting after his death before her wish was granted. Even then, I suspect, there was a wicked sense of humour at work. For, knowing that we were all living in the gathering suspense of waiting for her to complete her century, she died very quietly in her sleep one morning, a mere eight months before turning a hundred. I can still imagine her smiling up there somewhere, chuckling to herself and peacefully reciting:

We are such stuff
As dreams are made on, and our little life
Is rounded with a sleep.

André Brink was born in Vrede in the then Orange Free State. He grew up and went to school in several different villages and towns in South Africa: Vrede, Jagersfontein, Brits, Douglas, Sabie and Lydenburg. He is one of South Africa's leading novelists and is also an essayist, teacher and playwright. He writes in Afrikaans and English and is emeritus professor of English at the University of Cape Town.

Prince Mangosuthu Buthelezi

A GREAT ARTIST AND A GREAT SOUTH AFRICAN PATRIOT

Princess Magogo Mantithi Sibilile Thembisile Ngangezinye kaDinuzulu-Buthelezi, born 1900 in uSuthu, died 21 November 1984 in Durban

Princess Magogo, as she was more popularly known, was the daughter of King Dinuzulu and Queen Silomo okaNtuzwa kaMdlalose. She was the sister of King Solomon kaDinuzulu and Prince Mshiyeni kaDinuzulu.

King Dinuzulu was involved in a civil war between his followers uSuthu and Mandlakazi under one of the former generals of his father, Zibhebhu Zulu. As a result, King Dinuzulu was exiled to St Helena. He was still in his early twenties. Two of his wives were exiled with him, Queen Silomo and Queen Zihlanzile okaQethuka kaMagwaza. Two of my mother's brothers, whose names have already been given, were born on the island of St Helena during their father's exile. King Dinuzulu returned from exile in 1897. My mother, Princess Magogo, was born at the turn of the century during the Anglo-Boer War.

My grandmother died while my mother was still young. My mother used to tell us how she struggled to prepare food for her brothers at a young age. She only attended primary school.

When my mother was in her twenties her brother King Solomon asked her to marry Inkosi Mathole, my father. My father asked his people to give the lobolo (dowry) cattle for my mother. As the King's daughter, a hundred cattle had to be offered as lobolo. My mother got married to my father in 1926. It was not until 1928 that I was born as her first child. This was followed in 1932 by the birth of my sister, Princess Morgina, in 1932. In 1942 another daughter, Princess Admarah, was born.

My mother was a remarkable woman. She was brought up in the Anglican Church and was confirmed by one of the very first Diocesan bishops of the Diocese of Zululand, Bishop Vyvyan. AmaZulu have a tradition that, on the second day after the marriage of a daughter, both families, that is both the bride's people and the bridegroom's family, sit down before the bride's people depart. At this particular meeting the bride's people are given the opportunity to inform the groom's people about the state of health of their daughter. For instance, if she is constantly bothered by migraine or any other illness, this is disclosed to the groom's people. However, in the case of my mother, we are told that her people said that she was in perfect health, but the one thing she could not stop doing was singing. And, since a newly married bride may not sing in accordance with the Zulu custom of *ukuhlonipha*, her people were seeking a special dispensation for the Princess to be allowed to sing because for her singing was like a disease! She was a great musician and composer.

She played some Zulu instruments such as *ugubhu* (a Zulu musical bow attached to a bent stick with a string made of a strand from a horse's tail). She could also play the autoharp and could sing songs that go today under the name of *umbhaqanga*. She could also 'vamp' the piano and accompany herself singing Psalms of David. She could recite many of David's Psalms word for word in isiZulu when she conducted prayers. I remember in particular Psalm 91, which she recited word for word from the beginning to the end. It is known that she read the Zulu Bible from the beginning to the end three times in her lifetime.

President Thabo Mbeki bestowed on her the Ikamanga National Award (Gold Class) for her contribution to music.

I learned my politics on her knee. She would relate to me how the white soldiers arrived at uSuthu Royal Residence, her home, to arrest her father King Dinuzulu after the 1906 Zulu Rebellion. Her father was implicated by his agreeing to *give sanctuary* to Inkosi Bhambatha's wife Siyekiwe (uMaZuma) and his daughter Kholekile during that disturbance. The King was sentenced to life imprisonment. He was, however, released in 1910 by the first prime minister of South Africa, General Louis Botha, as he knew him as a friend before he got into trouble.

My mother was my great inspiration and gave me unstinting support throughout what has been a very trying and difficult political career. She did so until she reached the end of her days on 21 November 1984.

When I was about to do articles under a Durban lawyer, Rowley Israel Arenstein, it was my mother and leaders of the ANC such as Inkosi Albert Luthuli and Mr Oliver Tambo who said that my duty to the nation was to return from Durban to take my position as Inkosi of the Buthelezi clan. Because of my rustication from the University of Fort Hare, the government were not overly keen to recognise me as the hereditary Inkosi of the Buthelezi clan. My mother waged a very long and hard struggle to get me installed in April 1953, as Pretoria was so strongly against me because the government said that they could only recognise me as an acting Inkosi, even though this was my position by birth.

Although Princess Magogo was the tenth wife of my father, who had twenty wives, her status had been declared on the day of the marriage. The Zulu code decreed that the status of the Chief Wife of Inkosi must be declared on the day of her marriage. The other point was that when an Inkosi asks the clan for cattle for lobolo, he thereby contractually binds himself that the heir will come from her House. I remember that my mother sent one of my uncles with money for my bus fare and a demand that I must abandon my legal articles and return to take my position as the hereditary Inkosi of the Buthelezi clan. And that was not to be easily done. Pretoria was totally against it because of my involvement in the demonstration against the visit of the then governor general of South Africa, Dr G Brand van Zyl. On the other hand, my uncle, who was acting Inkosi since my father's death in 1942, was not overly keen to make way for me to take over. I remember Princess Magogo walking long distances to persuade my uncle to make way for me. I remember the long walks she took to the magistrate's office in Mahlabathini to make representations that I should now be recognised in my position as my father's successor Inkosi of the Buthelezi clan.

That was not to be the end of her woes. When the government decided to impose passes on African women, Princess Magogo led the opposition of women in Mahlabathini district. In 1957 Pretoria had decided to confirm my appointment as Inkosi of the Buthelezi clan. Princess Magogo again found herself between the devil and a hard place when Pretoria threatened not to confirm my appointment as Inkosi if she insisted on leading a demonstration that was due to take place at the magistrate's office in Mahlabathini.

In 2002, Opera Africa produced an opera based on the life of the Princess: *Princess Magogo kaDinuzulu*. The music was composed by that veteran composer Professor Mzilikazi Khumalo. The famous singer Sibongile Khumalo played my mother's role in the opera. She often states that she was inspired to be a singer herself by Princess Magogo. When Sibongile's father, Khabi Mngoma, was professor of music at the University of Zululand, Professor Mngoma and his family would sometimes stay with us. My mother would play her *ugubhu* musical bow and Sibongile would listen to her with members of her family. *Princess Magogo kaDinuzulu* has been a great success. It has been performed in Chicago and Oslo.

I am privileged to be the son of a mother who was not only a great artist but also a great South African patriot.

Prince Mangosuthu Buthelezi was born in Mahlabathini and grew up in Nongoma, KwaZulu-Natal. He is a Zulu leader and leader of the Inkatha Freedom Party. He was Minister of Home Affairs from 1994 to 2004 and has been a member of Parliament since 1994.

Yvonne Chaka Chaka

METI MNTAKA-NGWENYA (THE CHILD OF NGWENYA)

Nomakula Meti Sophie Ngwenya, born 12 January 1936 in Shalaston (Charliestown), died 28 April 2006 in Dobsonville

Nomakula Meti Sophie Ngwenya was one of ten children born to Sisi S and Sdintsi. She was the second child born into a modest family of Swazi heritage. Raised by her paternal grandmother, Maliyavuza, in Nigel, Meti later moved to Newcastle where she spent her teenage years brought up by her aunt and uncle, Ali and Vese Nyembe. Meti matured into a beautiful and hard-working woman.

One day a young man called Puti Habakuk 'Rex' Machaka came into Meti's life, and they got married. He was eighteen years her senior, and extremely handsome. Rex was also gifted with a melodious voice, but I remember Mom couldn't sing a note. They were blessed with three daughters: Skhumbuzo Doreen, Hendrica Refiloe and me, Moloko Yvonne. My father used to refer to Doreen as Maruping, a beautiful Pedi name. He would refer to Refiloe as Maputi, which was his mother's name. Often he would tenderly call her 'Mme'. Even though I was the youngest he would call me 'Gogo'. I loved this. I knew then that he was pleased with me.

We, the Machaka sisters, were a formidable group of girls. Fortunately our parents were also tough but fair. Mom was a very smart woman, and I realised this only in later life. I recall Fridays when my father would tell my mother not to cook. We would get very excited when we heard my father's distinctive whistle. He would bring a packet of fish and chips for each one of us. Every Saturday morning, without fail, dad would wake up early and make the fire in our coal-burning stove that every Sowetan resident owned. By the time we all woke up our breakfast was ready and served. Meti had taught Rex well. My father was a well-groomed husband who understood that he had to share the chores with his wife. He always found ways to make my mother feel like a special woman.

My parents were both quite special, and must have thought I was very entertaining. When I was little I would strum an empty tin and blow into a broomstick pretending it was a microphone. It seems I inherited talent from my father, so music is in my blood. I am blessed that I achieved what my father had not been able to accomplish.

One of my earliest memories of my mother was as a child when we lived in Newcastle. At daybreak my mother arrived home from Johannesburg, where she worked as a domestic worker. I could hear her footsteps in the early morning silence, around five a.m. As she arrived she discovered one of her brothers was just coming in. She chased him around the house wanting to know why he wasn't in bed asleep. She had a strong but loving personality, and she could bully even her big brothers when protecting their wives, who loved her dearly. Whenever they had problems with their husbands they knew they could depend on Meti to give the brothers a hiding. This attribute of strength and authority served my mother well, and she needed it on many occasions.

There were times when things were very difficult for our family. Mom had to go away briefly to live as a domestic in Florida where she worked for Philip and Pat Minaar, whose four young children Mom dearly loved. She adored them and demonstrated to them the same discipline and wisdom she provided her own children. At times all three of us would live with Mom in one small room in the back of the madam's house. During the week I would go to school in Dobsonville, and on weekends I would see my father who stayed in our house.

Mom worked very hard as a domestic but she had to supplement her salary to pay for our school fees and uniforms and to buy food and clothing, so she played *fafi*. Due to the fact that she had to work long hours we girls also had to learn how to play this peculiar game and understand the choreographed hand signals and secret codes in the numbers 1 to 36. Sometimes we had to take Mom's *fafi* bets for her and exchange them to the Chinese man sitting in his car parked on the corner of the all-white suburban neighbourhood. Sometimes she would win, and other times she would lose, but she never gave up. She was a tenacious mother who took her responsibilities seriously. Being poor taught me that every cent meant something, that everything you earned was important. I grew to understand why she had to resort to playing *fafi*.

When I was eleven years old something happened that would forever change my life. My father died. At the time, an unmarried woman was prevented from owning property in South Africa. Consequently, the government took action to confiscate our house from Meti. We had to move out and stay with my grandmother in Zondi for several years. During this time we were separated from our mother. My sisters and I had to sleep on the floor, and we were at the mercy of relatives.

We were blessed that Meti's employer, Pat, became our friend. She was amazing. She went into action: wrote letters on our behalf, went to court and wrestled with the authorities for our rights. She fought tooth and nail so that the government would not take our house away. I recall how my mother kept a positive attitude throughout this ordeal. She prayed that things would get better, that we would be reunited again to live as a family in our own house.

Eventually the government relented and allowed my mother to keep our family home. Although she no longer had her husband, and we no longer had our father, we still had our house. We eagerly moved back into the home that we loved so much. Mom smiled again.

At an early age I became a sickly child, and I experienced convulsions. This prompted my mother toward her spiritual quest to get me healed. She took me to numerous traditional healers. We went to many churches. Countless people laid hands on me, but nothing helped. Then, in 1975, my mother found God at the International Pentecostal Church led by Reverend Ntate Frederick Modise. Mom believed his prayers healed me, because from that time I never had another convulsion. Reverend Modise became a powerful presence in my mother's life. Her faith was resolute and unyielding. Meti loved her Lord and became a passionate servant to her Christian beliefs.

My sisters and I grew up in that church. Every Saturday we would go with my mother to attend prayer service. My sister, Refiloe, had a tremendous talent and became the choir leader. In due course, I too sang in the choir. That's where I discovered my voice. Ironically, it was Reverend Modise that predicted I would grow up to travel the world and sing for kings and queens. Little did I know that his prophecy would come true.

Mom knew I loved singing. I would even sing when I wasn't supposed to. She would often yell at me for making noise, and tell me to stop screaming. I didn't. As I reflect on this period of my life I realise that the church was our safe haven. It kept us girls out of mischief, and protected us from the dangerous unrest of our streets, where daily riots and protests against apartheid were taking place.

I remember how difficult those days were. We were a family of women only in a house without a man to protect us. I realise that my mother could have allowed us girls to run the streets and have boys come into our home. We could have been exploited as four vulnerable women. Anything could have happened to us, but Mom was a pillar of strength and discipline. Meti was a symbol of dignity to all who knew her. She was protective and determined, and knew that three pretty daughters could all too easily get lost in a world of desperation and immorality.

Life was always challenging for the Machaka family. My mother taught us that we had to be happy with the little we had. This was a hard lesson to learn as a teenager. We all wanted nice, new things, and she could not afford them. You could not bring anything into our house that she did not provide or approve. My eldest sister Doreen had to go to work at an early age, so she trained as a nurse. Her earnings exceeded Mum's entire salary, but Mom was so proud. Doreen was able to replace the earnings that were lost as a result of my father's death. It was at this time that I received my first-ever new item of clothing. Doreen bought me a jersey. I cherished and loved it. It was all mine, not a hand-me-down. Mom was pleased for me.

My mother was a modest woman, yet she was very straightforward. She did not fear giving her opinion to others, or to us. Doreen, who was the sweetest of us three rambunctious girls, would take her time to get chores done right. Mom was impatient and wanted things done quickly. She would say things like, 'Lomnenke-lo' ('You snail'), 'Wena, nenyeke yakho' ('You, with the big lips') or 'Ngiza kubamba' ('I will smack you'). If she were in a sarcastic mood then she would laugh, and say, 'Ha Hleka Mtaka Ngwenya' ('Ha, laugh child of Ngwenya'). Then we knew something was not right.

When she was happy she would say, 'Lekae' ('How are you') or 'Wari keing' ('What are you saying?') These words were said in an affectionate way that would melt any heart. Then she would make the best *idombolo* (dumplings) I've ever tasted. I never got the recipe or learnt how to make it, and now I wish I had. I recall with sadness that she would say, in her laughable, broken English, 'You should to make me coffee now!' I wish I could make her coffee now. In April 2007 she died. My life will never be the same again.

My mother insisted that all her daughters finish high school. She said, 'If I have to sell my last shoe, I will work to get you girls educated.' She knew high school would give us a foundation for a future education, even though she could never afford to send us to university. She wanted us to be better women, better people, to provide for ourselves and to contribute to society. She wanted me to become a lawyer, Doreen to become a doctor, and Refiloe to become an educated mother who would bear her six grandsons, because no boys had yet been born to our family. Destiny stepped in and, to her dismay, I began my singing career. Today, we are all professional women with tertiary educations. We are better women, better people. We provide for ourselves and contribute to society like she would have wanted.

Mom always washed and ironed our clothes until we left the house and went on our own. I suppose this is the reason I don't know how to iron my own clothes today. However, she taught us to clean a house well, and my helpers know that to this day I can still clean my own house.

When I became famous, Mom remained my best friend. She would call me to tell me when I had been on the news, she would collect magazine and newspaper articles, and she would insist that I cook for my husband and children. She believed in being a modern woman with rights, but she also honoured tradition and knew how important family was.

My mother taught us to love and respect ourselves despite the fact that we were poor, black and women. She often said that if you didn't love and respect yourself then no one else would. I know what it is like to go to bed without food. I know what it is like to be without. Her philosophy was to get on with things and not drown in your sorrows. She taught me that when you die you are not going to take anything with you. So when I have, I share with others.

Mom was my first mentor. It doesn't matter to me that she was a domestic with only a Standard Six education. Whatever she would have been, it would have been the best. Meti was a life-long teacher to all who knew her. She gave me the gift of character. Honesty, generosity, gratitude, faith, responsibility and moral integrity are all virtues my mother taught me. Mom was always there for me. What she went through as a young widow raising three daughters single-handedly on a domestic worker's salary took great courage and strength. The greatest praise I can give to my mother is that she encouraged me to get an education and reach my dreams. She was a responsible human being, she paid her debts and her word was her honour. The woman I am today is because of her. *Lala kahle Ntombi kaNgwenya, Mtimande, Bhambo Lunye* (Rest in peace).

Yvonne Chaka Chaka was born and grew up in Soweto. She became the first black child to appear on South African television in *Sugar Shack*, a national talent show in 1981. She is a singer who has been at the forefront of South African popular music for over twenty years. Her pan-African popularity led to her title 'Princess of Africa'.

Chris Chameleon

FAITH AND LOVE

Jolena Smit, born 14 May 1937 in Worchester

I am blessed with an amazing career and a life so wonderful it seems like fantasy. I do exactly what I love doing most and I am living my dream. But I can neither take these privileges for granted nor take all the credit for them. It took great sacrifice and unwavering dedication from my mother to enable this fortunate set of circumstances.

When I was only three weeks old, I lost my father and my mother found herself alone with no job, no money, no place to live and two babies to take care of. She bought a couple of dresses on account from Foschini in Johannesburg and set out to find a job. She was in luck and got a job as a secretary for a firm based in the city.

A Capetonian for most of her life, she looked at Johannesburg as an outsider would and judged it as only a lady of style and class could. She decided that she would settle in the affluent northern suburbs. Now this was an interesting decision, considering her financial situation, but she was thinking further into the future. She wanted her children to grow up in a privileged environment with exposure to the best education and a sophisticated social environment. This meant that I spent my childhood living in a little flat off Beyers Naudé Drive (back then it was DF Malan Drive), walked to school and was never able to compete with my peers when it came to toys or clothes. It would have been a whole lot easier if she had settled somewhere else, where living arrangements were more affordable and where we would blend in a bit better in our hand-me-down clothes (until this day I am still tempted to buy clothes that are a few sizes too big because I have become so used to it!) and with our home-made toys, but as I've said, she had a different plan.

We did get pocket money, my sister and I, for a total period of two weeks. The idea was that my sister would get eight cents, because she was eight, and I would get six cents, because I was six. But after two weeks I realised that my sister could buy two Kojack lollipops per week more than I could and I complained. My mother took this as a sign that I had finally come to understand the value of money and stopped giving it to us for free. From then on we had to work for it! When I turned thirteen I was allowed to start delivering newspapers and I had a twenty-one kilometre route for seventy-six newspapers that I had to wake up for at four-thirty every morning, six days a week, until my last school year.

My mother also never got involved in our troubles beyond the point of giving us emotional support and sound advice whenever we asked for it. She taught us that one has to fight one's battles alone and not drag others into it. She's an extremely proud individual who would ask favours from others only as a very last resort. She worked very hard, leaving before dawn and coming home after sunset.

Although some of this sounds a little tough, the truth is that I was showered with love throughout my childhood. I never felt that I wasn't loved and I was always very proud of my mom, even when I was a teenager when that sort of thing is rather difficult. Even then it was clear to me that my mother's principles added something to our lives that couldn't be quantified, and that this made us stand our ground in any situation under all sorts of circumstances. By the time I was a teenager I had discovered my wild side, the part of me that wanted to be a musician and never fitted in with the norm. These were trying times for my mother. But she just spent more time in prayer and held me to the values she had taught me.

She had an interesting way of not being involved yet still being supportive. I'm sure she really wanted me to 'go out and get a real job', but true to form she let me make my decisions and silently supported them in the faith that if I made them in the light of the virtues she had installed in me, they would turn out to my benefit. Probably her greatest service to my talents and dreams came after school. At an age when young people are expected to study further and/or get a career going, I chose to kiss my distinction-rich schooling career goodbye and focus on music. This meant that I became a dreamy young adult who slept until ten on weekday mornings and then got up to make a noise on my guitar. For a year this would be okay, two years at a stretch. But my mother tolerated this indulgence for almost ten years after school! Yep,

I intermittently lived under my mother's roof until I was about twenty-seven! This was in fact a very necessary privilege, for it gave me the time I needed to commit to music and acting and to develop these skills in the absence of mundane concerns.

It still took another seven years after I had left home to make a breakthrough in my career, the sort of breakthrough that has enabled me to look after not just my own needs, but also those of my mother and the people I employ today. My mother can now retire assured that I will take care of her needs for as long as either of us is alive and that I will remain dedicated to her well-being as a matter of priority. For I am grateful beyond expression for her support, her good judgement, her faith and her love that has been the single, greatest force of empowerment to my wonderful and privileged life.

Here's to you, Mom. I thank you from the bottom of my heart. I love you.

Chris Chameleon grew up in Johannesburg, in a flat off DF Malan Rylaan (now Beyers Naudé Drive). He was first known as an actor, winning South Africa's largest national acting competition in 1989. Today he is one of South Africa's top musicians. Currently a solo artist, he was the lead singer and bass guitarist for the band Boo!

JM Coetzee

THE BICYCLE

Vera Hildred Maria Coetzee (née Wehmeyer),
born 9 February 1904 on Diepkloof farm near
Avontuur in the upper Langkloof, close to
Uniondale, died 1985 in Rondebosch

They live on a housing estate outside the town of Worcester, between the railway line and the National Road. The streets of the estate have tree-names but no trees yet. Their address is No. 12 Poplar Avenue. All the houses on the estate are new and identical. They are set in large plots of red clay earth where nothing grows, separated by wire fences. In each back yard stands a small block consisting of a room and a lavatory. Though they have no servant, they refer to these as 'the servant's room' and 'the servant's lavatory.' They use the servant's room to store things in: newspapers, empty bottles, a broken chair, an old coir mattress.

At the bottom of the yard they put up a poultry-run and instal three hens, which are supposed to lay eggs for them. But the hens do not flourish. Rainwater, unable to seep away in the clay, stands in pools in the yard. The poultry-run turns into an evil-smelling morass. The hens develop gross swellings on their legs, like elephant-skin. Sickly and cross, they cease to lay. His mother consults her sister in Stellenbosch, who says they will return to laying only after the horny shells under their tongues have been cut out. So one after another his mother takes the hens between her knees, presses on their jowls till they open their beaks, and with the point of a paring-knife picks at their tongues. The hens shriek and struggle, their eyes bulging. He shudders and turns away. He thinks of his mother slapping stewing-steak down on the kitchen counter and cutting it into cubes; he thinks of her bloody fingers.

The nearest shops are a mile away along a bleak eucalyptus-lined road. Trapped in this box of a house on the housing estate, there is nothing for his mother to do all day but sweep and tidy. Every time the wind blows, a fine ochre clay-dust whirls in under the doors, seeps through the cracks in the window-frames, under the eaves, through the joints of the ceiling. After a day-long storm the dust lies piled inches high against the front wall.

They buy a vacuum cleaner. Every morning his mother trails the vacuum cleaner from room to room, sucking up the dust into the roaring belly on which a smiling red goblin leaps as if over a hurdle. A goblin: why?

He plays with the vacuum cleaner, tearing up paper and watching the strips fly up the pipe like leaves in the wind. He holds the pipe over a trail of ants, sucking them up to their death.

There are ants in Worcester, flies, plagues of fleas. Worcester is only ninety miles from Cape Town, yet everything is worse here. He has a ring of fleabites above his socks, and scabs where he has scratched. Some nights he cannot sleep for the itching. He does not see why they ever had to leave Cape Town.

His mother is restless too. I wish I had a horse, she says. Then at least I could go riding in the veld. A horse! says his father: Do you want to be Lady Godiva?

She does not buy a horse. Instead, without warning, she buys a bicycle, a woman's model, second-hand, painted black. It is so huge and heavy that, when he experiments with it in the yard, he cannot turn the pedals.

She does not know how to ride a bicycle; perhaps she does not know how to ride a horse either. She bought the bicycle thinking that riding it would be a simple matter. Now she can find no one to teach her.

His father cannot hide his glee. Women do not ride bicycles, he says. His mother remains defiant. I will not be a prisoner in this house, she says. I will be free.

At first he had thought it splendid that his mother should have her own bicycle. He had even pictured the three of them riding together down Poplar Avenue, she and he and his brother. But now, as he listens to his father's jokes, which his mother can meet only with dogged silence, he begins to waver. Women don't ride bicycles: what if his father is right? If his mother can find no one willing to teach her, if no other housewife in Reunion Park has a bicycle, then perhaps women are indeed not supposed to ride bicycles.

Alone in the back yard, his mother tries to teach herself. Holding her legs out straight on either side, she rolls down the incline toward the chicken-run. The bicycle tips over and comes to a stop. Because it does not have a crossbar, she does not fall, merely staggers about in a silly way, clutching the handlebars.

His heart turns against her. That evening he joins in with his father's jeering. He is well aware what a betrayal this is. Now his mother is all alone.

Nevertheless she does learn to ride, though in an uncertain, wobbling way, straining to turn the heavy cranks.

She makes her expeditions to Worcester in the mornings, when he is at school. Only once does he catch a glimpse of her on her bicycle. She is wearing a white blouse and a dark skirt. She is coming down Poplar Avenue toward the house. Her hair streams in the wind. She looks young, like a girl, young and fresh and mysterious.

Every time his father sees the heavy black bicycle leaning against the wall he makes jokes about it. In his jokes the citizens of Worcester interrupt their business to stand and gape as the woman on the bicycle labours past. *Trap! Trap!* they call out, mocking her: Push! There is nothing funny about the jokes, though he and his father always laugh together afterwards. As for his mother, she never has any repartee, she is not gifted in that way. 'Laugh if you like,' she says.

Then one day, without explanation, she stops riding the bicycle. Soon afterwards the bicycle disappears. No one says a word, but he knows she has been defeated, put in her place, and knows that he must bear part of the blame. I will make it up to her one day, he promises himself.

The memory of his mother on her bicycle does not leave him. She pedals away up Poplar Avenue, escaping from him, escaping towards her own desire. He does not want her to go. He does not want her to have a desire of her own. He wants her always to be in the house, waiting for him when he comes home. He does not often gang up with his father against her: his whole inclination is to gang up with her against his father. But in this case he belongs with the men.

From *Boyhood*

JM Coetzee was born in Cape Town. On his father's side he is descended from Dutch settlers dating to the seventeenth century. Coetzee also has Polish roots, as his great-grandfather was a Polish immigrant to South

Africa. He spent most of his early life in Cape Town and in Worcester in the Western Cape Province. He is a novelist, literary critic and academic, and won the Nobel Prize for Literature in 2003.

Nelle Dreyer

THE STORY OF THE SILVER SPOON

Nelle van Dyk, born 1922 in Vereeniging

I wish I could hug you right now.

Your voice sounded faint tonight. 'I'm eighty-five, it's normal to have an off day at my age,' you said. Of course, Ma, it's normal. You're exceptional for your age, as beautiful and dignified as ever, as enthusiastic and positive about all I tell you ... I want you to know that as I am sitting here at my desk in Paris, you're with me. You're always with me. And I know that thousands of miles away, you know that I'm there with you.

For how long you remember our conversations, I don't know, but I cling to every morsel of advice you give me, every morsel of truthful criticism you throw at me and every morsel of faith you have in me.

I listen when you describe what it is like to have memory lapses. Blanks. That you're aware of it and how frightening it is. And I know you tell me these things only because I ask you, not to complain or because you expect me to rush home, but to quiet my curiosity of how it feels, of what one goes through, so that I may understand.

You have always explained things to me.

How I love your remarkable gift of mixing reality with fantasy or fantasy with spirituality. Do you remember the day you taught me about wishing? I was six years old. You were watering the garden ...

'Nelletjie, have I told you the story of our silver spoon?'

'Huh-uh.'

'The big serving-spoon we use every day ... when we moved into this house, we moved in with very little, even without a serving-spoon. I wanted one so badly, so I started wishing every day, at every meal time. I did not wish for an ordinary spoon either; it had to be silver.'

'And then?'

'Then, weeks later, while I was planting these flowers, the ones I'm watering right now, right here, what do you think I discovered in the ground?'

'The silver spoon!'

'Precisely! And what does that teach you?'

'I don't know.'

'It teaches you that you can have anything you wish for.'

'Anything?'

'Yes, if you know what you want and if you wish for it with your entire soul. And you have to believe.'

You were right, Ma. When one wishes with the soul and believes, the wish comes true. It might take years, but it does come true.

You taught me to believe.

Yes, Ma, because you believed in me, I believed in myself, believed in life, believed that everything is possible. Positive thinking, you called it. Positive thinking is what people write books about these days; you applied it fifty years ago.

You were interested in the re-conditioning of thinking patterns. You treated and cured your patients of anxiety and neurosis. You cured my depression at puberty. 'Stop dwelling on yourself,' you told me. 'Look at nature, the wonders of creation, smell the air, listen to the birds, the wind, the rain … touch a flower.' You took me to visit the botanical gardens in Constantia. We had tea there while my friends sat in the classroom. You explained that unless I decided to get myself out of the negative thinking spiral, you were incapable of helping me. 'You are the master of your own destiny,' you told me. 'Stop feeling sorry for yourself.'

Do you remember the Tarzan food? Tarzan food, Ma, is what you fed us as children. It was shredded raw spinach topped with grated carrots, sliced tomatoes, crushed garlic with an olive oil and orange juice dressing to make it more palatable. 'This is exactly what Tarzan eats to be as strong as he is.' Oh, we struggled to get the rabbit food down our throats, but we did, because we believed you. And later, when we knew it was only a story, we ate it nevertheless; there was nothing else. And thank God there was nothing else – no white bread, no cooldrinks, no cakes or biscuits or sweets. We grew up as healthy children, Vanlier and I. You saw to it. And today I know about nutrition.

You were ahead of your time, Ma.

I remember your efforts to introduce exercise breaks and balanced diets into the daily routine of office-workers in the early sixties … in the schools as well. You believed nutrition should be part of the school curriculum. Well, Ma, the minister of health might have smiled with scepticism at the time, but rest assured – no minister of health smiles sceptically any longer.

Where your wisdom comes from baffles me: 'A human being needs to develop on six different levels: the physical, the cultural, the intellectual, the spiritual, the emotional and the social level.' This was your philosophy of what it takes to be a balanced human being.

I have strived to be that balanced person. The natural beauty I was given at birth did not alter me, though it could have. My career as a model could have distorted my values, but it did not. I could have been a failure at business with my husband; I wasn't. I could have been a hopeless wife. As Bob says, 'I married you for your integrity, not your beauty.' Thanks to you, Ma.

But how did *you* find out about these things?

Your mother never enlightened you; you say she stifled you. You were born in 1922 and grew up in small villages and farms. Your father started as a railway clerk – an Afrikaans family of no significant background. You had no girlfriends to discuss your thoughts with; even Pa was uninterested in your theories.

How did you learn about teaching the deaf and dumb children at St Mary's School to move on the beat of music by feeling the vibrations with their bare feet on the floorboards?

Who taught you to manage a car hire business and become a master at marketing? Marketing! Hardly anyone even knew the word in South Africa at the start of the sixties.

And then the English cucumbers. You imported the seeds, read all the agricultural manuals in French – translated it, without knowing the language! You were the pioneer of English cucumbers in South Africa, Ma.

And in-between you taught me to be an individual.

We always speak about our relationship, how special it is, how close we are. Again tonight you mentioned how there is no resentment between us, no prejudice, no expectations, no blame, no suffocation.

No guilt, Ma – for the absence of guilt I thank you every day.

Do you realise that more than half of my life has been spent away from you and that despite being apart, we have grown closer? Of course you do.

I wonder how another mother would have reacted with her only daughter living abroad. Would she have been content with one visit per year? Would a phone call every Sunday have sufficed? Would she have been as proud of me, as happy for me, without reproach, as unselfishly as you have been?

A long time ago, four years into my marriage, I called you in desperation, saying that I could no longer go on, that Bob was too egotistical and never gave me any credit as a business partner. That our life together was one big struggle without money, that the French were abominable, our apartment still in shambles … I remember how miserable I was. I wanted to hear you agree with me, to tell me to pack my bags.

Instead, you rebuked, encouraged and complimented me in the same breath: 'Are you giving enough from your side, or are you merely expecting things to come to you? If you give more, you will get more … and if anybody knows about giving, it's you.'

I didn't like it, but nevertheless thought you were right. You were always right. Okay, I said, so I'm not giving enough and I know that marriage has its ups and downs, as you've always told me. 'Just tell me one thing,' I asked you. 'How long can a down-period last?' The silence was so long, I thought you had hung up. 'Ma? Are you still there?'

'Of course,' you said, 'I'm thinking … about five years!'

How right you were. It did take five years, five difficult years, precious years of learning how to persevere, how to give, how to concede, to forgive, to acknowledge, to humour, to appreciate …

You are the strong one. You could have had me back, you could have said 'You're right, France is not your home, come home.' But you thought of me, not yourself.

You gave me freedom. You allowed me to fly. You wanted me to fly, to live life as I chose.

My every wish has come true.

How do you put it?

'Life is in the invisible – it's not what we do, it's how we think.'

Nelle Adamski Dreyer was born in Stellenbosch and became South Africa's first international *Vogue* model in the seventies. She lives in Paris and is married to Robert (Bob) Adamski, a Polish-American graphic designer. In 1983 she launched the Nelle Dreyer *prêt-à-porter* label. She is managing director of Adamski designs and manages their gallery space in Paris. She is also a digital artist.

Diana Ferrus

A POWERFUL TONGUE

Anna Fransina Ferrus (nèe Elias), born
5 March 1926 in Worcester

'Speak up,' she said. 'One day when you land in trouble I will not be there to help you. Then you will have to speak for yourself, so learn to speak!' And how did she speak, how many times did she speak for me, reprimand me and even shame me.

My mother, Anna Fransina Ferrus (née Elias) was born on 5 March 1926 in the scenic Boland town of Worcester. Her father, Marinus Elias, was her hero. He was a great sportsman who excelled in cricket and rugby. His nickname was 'Bokkie Mariens', so called by a doctor Luyt who came to watch him play cricket and told him: 'You should have been a Springbok!' My mother inherited his personality and his talent. She was her school's sprint and long-jump champion. After she had left school, the principal begged her to represent his school at some championships in Green Point, Cape Town. She was defiant and scoffed at any restrictions placed on her. She was the perfect rebel in an apartheid society deeply rooted in patriarchy.

My mother seemed not to be politically conscious but she hated to be treated unequally. She knew the law and how far she could go. One evening after a domestic quarrel, or rather a fight with my father, she went to lay a complaint. The police were not interested and she went straight to the mayor's house. She demanded that he reprimand the police. Of course she later withdrew the charges, but she did teach my father a lesson. This is also how she protected her female friends. She could be friend and foe alike. One man, a teacher, who physically abused his wife, was himself a victim of my mother's wrath when she hit him after he slapped his wife. He did not stop abusing his wife, but was very scared when my mother was around.

This young woman with the many dreams was temporarily knocked down by life's challenges. She married a battle-scarred soldier upon his return from a POW camp in Europe after the Second World War. He was not able to realise the dreams that she had for him and her. She did not understand what he himself could not understand. So they sank into a deep pit of alcohol abuse and many times put their children to shame. Yet, and in spite of the fact that my mother barely survived on the meagre income of my father who struggled to keep a job, we never went hungry.

She was the greatest cook and could create hearty meals from the simplest of foods. She was a perfectionist who taught us to wash, iron and clean properly. My mother never bought on credit and worked wisely with the little money she had. I became the avid reader she was. As a young girl I lay next to her and we read from the same book. She read faster than me and many a time had to wait before turning the page because I was not yet done. Both she and my father loved poetry and recited poems to us. Today I am a poet and writer. I spend money wisely and hate to buy on credit. Even though I did not turn out to be a great cook, I do excel in frying fish and making soup, two of her specialities.

I have many friends and I treat both adults and children with respect – traits she instilled in me. And when flashes of the hard times in our life threaten to ruin my day, I think of how she lifted herself from that pit. Then I think of how she tried to make up for the times she was not herself. And she did. Now in my adult life I realise that no one else has ever looked at me with such love-filled eyes.

My mother and I grew closer after the death of my father. This was when I truly discovered who she was, what she went through and how remarkable she was. Many times I think of the shame I felt when my mother was drunk, times when I thought she ought to have kept quiet. But today I am grateful that she spoke. My mother did not allow her family to harbour secrets – everything had to be out in the open. It did bring shame at the time, but today I have nothing to hide, thanks to her. In 1994 we voted together. How appropriate that we could take our first steps of freedom together. Here is to my mother who still speaks, but through me.

That day

On April twenty-seven, nineteen-ninety-four,
I took my mother's hand
for it was a new day in our land.
She was sixty-eight and I was forty-one
and as the morning sun made its daily run
we walked slowly, step by step.
The roads were abuzz but our minds were clear,
a new day in our lives was here.

On wobbly legs she entered the hall
but with head held high she suddenly looked so tall.
I watched as she made her cross,
as we regained the dignity that we had lost.

That day on April twenty-seven, nineteen-ninety-four
I took my mother's hand, for it was a new day in our land.

Diana Ferrus was born and grew up in Worcester as the third-born of six children. She is a poet who writes in both English and Afrikaans. She is well known for her poems about Saartjie Baartman and is also a founding member of Bush Poets, a women poets group at the University of the Western Cape where she works as an administrator.

Pam Golding

'BE NICE!'

Leila Edith Frances Robertshaw, born
5 January 1902 in Port Elizabeth,
died 6 May 1974 in Cape Town

Today, being a Sunday, was to be a lazy relaxed day listening to the wonderful classical and jazz programmes of Richard Jewson on Fine Music Radio and settling down to collect my thoughts and memories of my mother.

After listening to the music from the film *Out of Africa*, Mozart's Clarinet Concerto, Puccini's 'Oh My Beloved Father' (which made me think of my beloved mother), 'Rhapsody and Variations on a Theme by Paganini' and finally the beautiful, romantic and haunting music of Romance del Diablo, I had such a yearning for her that my tears flowed and my heart ached simply to talk to her and express to her how much I appreciated what she had done for me during her life.

When I was asked to write about my mother and the influence she had on my life, I wondered how I could possibly find the time in today's frenetic and busy world to do so. Today it is virtually impossible to fulfil the role of wife, mother, grandmother and businesswoman. There just isn't the time – it's crazy. It was never like that in my mother's day. It was somehow very different. One had the time to just 'be', to live, to play and to think. I've had to find the time to think about my mother and her life, and what a wonderful, emotional and exciting journey it has been!

My mother, Leila Edith Frances Robertshaw, was born on 5 January 1902 in Port Elizabeth. She was the second daughter to my grand-mother Florence, sister to Ailene and her brother Crobie. After Charles Robertshaw, my grandfather (a respected wool broker), died, my grand-mother remarried and had three more children, Jack, Rhona and Esmé. I mention this because my grandmother had quite a hard life and my mother, who was a champion swimmer and represented Eastern Province, had to leave school to look after the three younger children – no nannies, governesses or au pairs in those days, just a mother who brought up six children and was indeed greatly respected – a brave lady. She told hysterically funny stories of their old house in Cuyler Street where every corner was used. She used to let rooms to 'borders' and look after 'blind Aunty Lucy'; she turned the huge old dining-room table upside down and filled it with pillows and blankets to make another cosy place for the children to sleep.

I used to love listening to my mother's stories of her earlier days as a 'flapper' (the 1920s and dancing the Charleston, the short dresses, high-heeled shoes, bobbed hair with a fringe). She and her sister were considered to be the belles of Port Elizabeth. She loved dancing and her descriptions of the Port Elizabeth 100 Club Ball were so entertaining. The beautiful frocks they wore were designed and made by themselves. She was an excellent seamstress. In fact, she made most of my special evening dresses and ball gowns throughout my debutante years at school and university.

I remember her stories of various romances and proposals of marriage from suitors who wanted to marry her, until finally my father Henry Peter Munro Stroebel (called Timothy or Tim by his friends) asked her to marry him. He was a teacher at Grey High School in Port Elizabeth and was considered quite a catch. He was a great sportsman, motorbike racer and very handsome, which made him a very popular teacher.

They married on 13 December 1923 and were married for fifty-two years. She had a 'Society' wedding in PE hosted by Mr Arthur Phillip and his wife in their beautiful home. He was a well-known businessman, whom I subsequently got to know as Uncle Arthur when I was a student at UCT, by this time a darling man well into his nineties. He always adored my mother and was very special to me.

After my parents' marriage and the birth of their son Barry, they moved to Umtata, the capital of the old Transkei where my father was the senior school Afrikaans teacher and deputy headmaster for many years.

During the Second World War, the headmaster, Frank Baker, joined the forces and was captured in Tobruk, becoming a prisoner of war for the duration. My father was then appointed as headmaster and later retired in 1948. After his retirement he continued to play a very active role in the school athletics, sports and cadets.

My parents were a very popular couple and participated in amateur theatre, ballroom dancing championships, golf competitions, fishing trips and competitive bridge. My mother was an excellent bridge player. Both of them were accomplished pianists and my father also played the piano accordion extremely well. My mother loved singing. Oh, the memories of our Sunday evening family gatherings around the piano. They were legendary!

We had an extremely happy childhood – not in a material sense, but we participated in everything that went on in a small town like Umtata: sports, ballet, theatre, community events, charity functions, Women's Institute, Girl Guides, child welfare and concerts in aid of war funds.

As a family we had wonderful holidays at the Wild Coast where we owned a small holiday house with two thatched rondavels called a 'camp' to which we invited our school friends and the parents of special friends. My mother sold her DKW motor vehicle to pay for this holiday house made of corrugated iron and wood. It was at Sinangwana and, to quote my father, 'it had the finest sea views and beaches in the world.' We grew up in a completely unspoilt, beautiful area with excellent fishing. No electricity, only oil lamps, candles and a wood stove.

I remember how my mother catered for all of us with no supermarket nearby and no domestic help, yet we lived like kings. We caught lots of fish and never had to 'dress up' as we lived in bathing costumes and shorts. What a life that was. We were fortunate to have holidays four times a year because of my father being a teacher. What fun!

I recall that we had a radiogram in a large old cabinet which we wound up to play lots of 'His Master's Voice' records. No TV, no long-playing records, no DVDs or videos! We played card games and learnt to dance. Our life was outdoors, not indoors, it was very simple and best of all, lots and lots of fun.

My mother encouraged me to learn to play the piano, to study for music exams and to learn ballet. I continued with music throughout my school life. In fact, I played at school concerts and took music as a subject for matric. Today I don't play much, but our whole family, including my husband (who is a jazz pianist of note), children and grandchildren, are all very musical and play the piano, violin and guitar.

Our sons both have excellent voices and are sought after at our national conferences and parties to sing popular jazz pieces such as Frank

Sinatra's 'My Way' and 'Fly Me to the Moon'. I am also sometimes called upon at women's conferences at our home to sing my favourite tune, 'The Nearness of You', nightclub style. And so … back to my mother.

She was undoubtedly the most wonderful woman and mother, totally unselfish, kind, loving, generous, talented and brave. There is no doubt that she is my inspiration to be unafraid to accept challenges, never to be arrogant or unkind and to remain humble. In fact, our family motto is 'Be nice!' That motto was always adhered to whenever possible. She was a great companion to me and a lot of fun to be with.

When I was twenty-one, I made enough money, through selling memberships to the Junior Literary Society and volumes of books called *The Treasure Casket*, to earn sufficient commission to treat my mother to her first overseas holiday to London and Europe, and what a treat that was!

We sailed cabin class on the Union Castle Line. Buses, trains and bicycles were our means of transport. We stayed in various pensions. She loved the theatre, touring and wandering around flea markets such as Petticoat Lane, Portobello Road and the Arcades – 'Just looking' as we were very short of cash.

We were having such fun and enjoying ourselves so much, but had literally run out of money, so my mother sold a trunk full of our boring tweed clothes and long evening dresses to a second-hand clothing store to raise funds to stay a little longer! I can picture her now running down the street in South Kensington waving the cash in her hand with jubilation.

We took a tour of France, Italy and Switzerland, swimming on the French Riviera, gambling in Monaco, climbing mountains in Interlaken, wining and dining in Italy; we never had a dull moment. We both loved meeting people; she was as much an adventuress as I was at the age of twenty-one.

We met a group of Swiss yodellers at a ball at the Sorbonne in Paris who invited us to Switzerland. That's where we hired bicycles as our mode of transport.

My mother made the best of everything. She was innovative (today you would call her an entrepreneur) – nothing was too difficult for her to tackle. She had to work to help keep three children in expensive boarding schools and, unlike today, it was not fashionable for a mother to work. We lacked nothing, although we did not have many material things. They weren't important to us – we had a great childhood. We were successful in school as well as at sports and had a very happy family life of togetherness and fun.

My mother was a leader. It was she who organised functions to raise funds for the war effort. She started the amateur theatrical society and participated. She was the Lady Captain of the Golf Club, taught bridge, was a wonderful cook and made all my clothes. She raised monies for charities by teaching dancing and convening concerts. Many of her pupils still remember her shows. The interesting thing is that, at school, I learnt ballet and tap and it is I who taught her to dance so that she could teach her pupils!

She joined the army as a corporal in the Special Signals Division of SAWAS. If I hadn't been a schoolgirl during the war, I too would have joined up! She was a great saleswoman. She opened a boutique and was very successful. She also sold for the National Thrift Organisation and held meetings in the then Orange Free State to encourage people to save.

Even after having a stroke, which partially paralysed her left arm, she remained undaunted, and in my father's retirement, she tried farming and enjoyed secretarial opportunities with doctors in Cape Town and at the Bay View Hotel in Hermanus. She also made and sold iced Christmas cakes for charity.

She was an inspiration to me as a daughter. She never complained and never said an unkind word about anyone. She was great fun, loved to entertain and was my total confidante. She understood me perfectly and encouraged me to be independent and to make the most of life. Her mottos were 'Get on with it' and 'Have no regrets.' She was loved by everyone who came into contact with her. She spread joy wherever she went. She made enormous sacrifices for our family and was determined that I would get a university degree. She took a job behind the counter at Whitakers Store in Port St John's for a year when we were going through hard times and could not pay the doctor's bills.

In between all these activities was a mother ... a wonderful mother. Always there to comfort, advise and sympathise when we had lost dear friends and always helping others even when she herself was old and frail. She never complained or became bitter. She was indeed a true

Christian, loved and adored by all who knew her. The one sadness in her life was when my brother Deneys died suddenly of a heart attack at the age of forty-five. She was staying with us in Kenilworth at the time and I had to break the tragic news to her. I remember her words: 'To lose a son is the saddest day in my life.'

What a privilege it was for me to have Leila Edith Frances as a mother and friend. She too was a kind, thoughtful and loving daughter to her mother. My grandmother, travelling alone by tram, would visit me in boarding school in Port Elizabeth, despite the cold wind and rain, just to bring me a little treat. She was well into her seventies by then and when I was homesick, would say, 'Now Pam, pull yourself together and chin up, my darling.'

I remember some of my mother's wise sayings so well:

Count your blessings, Darling.
Remember the starving Poles – eat your vegetables.
Stick to your principles.
Think of others less privileged than you.
Don't have any regrets.
Be thankful for small mercies.
Stay on the dance floor – keep dancing and you'll stay out of trouble!

My love of property and decorating houses I inherited, I think, from my mother who had a talent for creating a 'home' in each house we lived in – and there were many that we rented over the years. She created gardens out of stony plots, she upholstered chairs, painted cupboards, draped fabrics and hunted for bargains. Our houses were mostly 'old style' with character, high ceilings and large sash windows. I subconsciously imbibed her flair, tastes and fondness for old furniture, antiques and characterful houses.

When my mother died in Groote Schuur hospital at seven p.m. on Sunday, 6 May 1974, I was with her, sitting at her bedside. She was sitting on the side of the bed swinging her legs in the new nightie I had just bought for her. She looked beautiful; in fact, she looked amazing, so young – not a line on her lovely face. I stared at her beauty as she begged me to take her home. I had agreed with her doctor that she could come home with me the next morning.

She bent down, put her arms around me and said, 'Darling, what would I have done without you,' and then fell back in the bed and died. What greater and closer moment could a mother and daughter have than that?

I have all these wonderful memories of my mother. She lived her life to the full and when I hear my mother's favourite music or songs, such as 'Just a Song at Twilight' and 'Ah Sweet Mystery of Love', my heart is filled with nostalgia; but as my grandmother used to say 'Chin up, Darling.' I look around at my beautiful home, filled with family treasures in a display cabinet in the living room with some of my mother's favourite things and family heirlooms; I am so grateful for the wonderful, loving memories!

If my children have the total respect, friendship, loyalty and warmth for me that I had for my mother – then I feel I will have achieved all I want for them. If I have given them that, then I will be totally satisfied that I have done a good job as a mother.

She had a devoted and loving family and many loyal friends, and there is not a day that goes by that I don't miss her and long to have all the years I had with her all over again.

Pamela 'Pam' Golding grew up in the then small town of Umtata in the Eastern Cape and was named one of the 50 leading women entrepreneurs in the world by The Star Group in 1998. She heads the Pam Golding Property Group which has 140 branches and 1600 personnel.

Richard Goldstone

PRODUCE THE BEST OF WHICH YOU
ARE CAPABLE

Catherine Phyllis Rene Jacobson, born
29 March 1912 in Benoni

My mother, Kitty Goldstone (born Catherine Phyllis Rene Jacobson), was born in Benoni on 29 March 1912. Happily she is still alive and well as she approaches her ninety-seventh birthday. My father was killed in a road accident ten years ago when he was ninety-one years of age. My mother lives alone and enjoys an active social life with her family and friends. She attended school at the Boksburg Convent where, after matriculating, she continued for some years to teach elocution, ballet and drama. When she was eighty-nine years old, she addressed the students at the Convent and told them about her school days.

I was an only child until the age of twenty. My parents then very surprisingly produced a second boy, David, who was only four years old when I married. One consequence was that my mother acquired new friends a generation younger than herself who had children the same age as my brother.

My mother encouraged me to listen to and understand classical music and that gift has played an important role in my life. I always work with music in the background and the benefit of countless hours of enjoyment is impossible to quantify.

Although not politically active, my mother always strongly opposed racial discrimination and was overjoyed that she survived to witness the end of apartheid. Her principle activity outside the home was working as a volunteer for philanthropic organisations. It was not surprising, therefore, that she encouraged me when, as a student at Witwatersrand University, I became active in anti-apartheid student government and the National Union of South African Students. Attempts by the Security Police to dissuade me from continuing with my political involvement in no way lessened her support of my activities.

My mother has always taken a keen interest in politics and sport. Still today she listens to the news many times a day and is always well up on the affairs of the day, both domestic and international. Her eyesight no longer enables her to read and she has adapted well to listening to the wonderful books provided to her by Tape Aids for the Blind. She spends no time on fiction, preferring to read history and philosophy. She has recently completed a book on the philosophy of Smuts and a biography of Winston Churchill.

I have no doubt that much of my success can be attributed to my mother's influence and, in particular, to her instilling in me a work ethic and a will to produce the best of which I am capable. She encouraged my successes as a child and her encouragement played an important role in my determination to succeed in whatever I undertook.

My mother now has four great-grandsons – three of them live near her in Johannesburg. She spends much time with them and is giving them similar benefits to those she gave to me. Her memory for details, long past and most recent, enables her to impart knowledge relating to literature, music and world affairs. Her interest in sport, especially tennis and cricket, makes her a thoroughly modern person and helps her to relate to young people. Her great-grandsons know that she can always give them the latest cricket score!

Richard Goldstone grew up in a Jewish household in Johannesburg. He studied at the University of the Witwatersrand and was elected president of the Student Representative Council in 1959. He is a judge, international war crimes prosecutor and one of the world's most respected jurists. He received the International Human Rights Award of the American Bar Association and the Thomas J Dodd Prize in International Human Rights. He served as a judge of the South African Constitutional Court from 1994 to 2003. In 2008 he was the second recipient of the MacArthur Foundation International Justice Award. The first was Kofi Annan.

Shaun Johnson

FAIRNESS IN LIFE

Joan Norma Johnson (née Storey), born 6 July
1921 in Benoni, died 5 April 2002 in Hermanus

My mother was really tiny. I mean really, really tiny, like a sparrow chick; she looked like she could be blown in to the air by a light breeze. My father was tall, nearly six foot, and my mother barely made five. When they walked together it was easier for him to lay his hand on her head than to put his arm around her shoulders. And like so many people who are very small, she packed the personality of a heavyweight, expressed it with the tongue of a Venus flytrap and was in her way much stronger than him.

My mom, Joan Norma Johnson (née Storey), who passed away in 2002 in her seventies after years of ill health, was born in Benoni long before the Campari joke. She always defended Benoni, said the people there had *good values*. (By this she meant unlike those big city slickers down the road in Johannesburg, where she was in fact to end up after years of southern African peripateticism, loyally following my civil servant father around on his extreme wanderings.)

She was part of the Benoni English, who were in fact surprisingly English, and though her large family was poor they were highly literate and spoke beautifully. Her grammar was immaculate, from her I first inherited a love of books and writing, and the ripest word I ever heard her use was 'ruddy'. For her that was swearing, so something must have made her very angry indeed.

She had it tough right from the start, and came very early to expect that life was meant to be tough, that this was the way of the world. She could not bear it when one of her sons complained about his lot. She dreamt as a girl of becoming a ballerina but fell ill and was too slight and too frail. As a young woman and wife she started a library in Kentani, in the old Transkei, but was never allowed to stay long enough in one place to become what she would have called a *proper* librarian, her second unfulfilled dream. When my dad died very young and in heartbreaking circumstances, leaving her with four boys and a minuscule government pension, she consciously rejected as an indulgence the idea of any further dreams for herself and did whatever piecework she could find to keep the family going.

From the age of forty she quite literally gave her life to the well-being of her sons. There was never another man for her though this was not because of a lack of suitors – she was pretty and stylish in the manner of the times, but one by one they gave up on her. She extracted a price from us for this sacrifice: her sons knew what she was having to forgo for their sakes – because she told us. She did guilt effectively.

She was a ruthless Scrabble fiend, a formidable bridge player, a reader above all, and every evening she would play her records and have a 'spot'. A highlight of her life was seeing Engelbert Humperdinck live at the Jo'burg Civic Centre. She flew on an aeroplane twice in her life – once to get to Europe and once to get back, the single 'Overseas Trip' for which she and my dad had saved for ten years, and which loomed large in our family folklore.

Her tongue could cut. This was not pleasant for those on the receiving end, but often it was memorably witty for she was an extremely clever person in spite of having left school early because of family finances. Late in her life, after yet more heart surgery, she found herself recovering in a crowded and somewhat chaotic hospital ward in Johannesburg. She had refused all our pleas to transfer her to a private ward – an unconscionable waste of scarce money, in her immovable view – but retained the right to complain about her circumstances. When I visited with my wife-to-be, my mother pulled herself up on to her pillows, looked at us, then raked the room with her eyes. Her stage whisper could be heard by all: 'Not a brain cell in the ward,' she pronounced. We collapsed laughing, and so did she.

I often thought later about her combined beliefs in fairness and fatalism. She was not political as my father was – on Politics with a capital P she would defer to him – but she held to a fiercely rigid moral code that she summarised as *fairness in life*. Every human being should be treated with equal dignity, wealth was not an indicator of good breeding, one should never be in debt, and one should pay one's taxes precisely on time and to the penny. Beyond that one might be allowed some fun, if it had been worked for.

Regarding her fatalism, I concluded that rather like Joseph Conrad's Russians in *Under Western Eyes*, her approach was that one should *expect* every day to be a struggle to avert imminent catastrophe – and thus appreciate it much more than Westerners when something nice happened. The result was that I think she wasn't happy very often in her life, but when she was, she was *really* happy. It is those times I like to remember when I think of her, which is often.

Shaun Johnson is a South African writer. He grew up in the then Transkei and Johannesburg and studied at Rhodes University and the University of Oxford, where he was a Rhodes Scholar. A journalist and newspaper editor for many years, he became founding chief executive of The Mandela Rhodes Foundation in 2003. He lives with his wife and daughter in Cape Town.

Farida Karodia

A WOMAN OF SUBSTANCE

Mary Elizabeth Petersen, born 25 January
1913 in Aliwal North, died 26 February 2007
in Calgary, Canada

It has taken ages for me to write this piece about my mother – not only because her death is still so fresh in my memory, but because it is difficult to find a starting point that encapsulates a life that spanned ninety-four years.

My mother, Mary Elizabeth Petersen, was born on 25 January 1913 in Aliwal North. However, I have decided to use as my starting point the latter half of her life, since this is the period that holds my most vivid memories of her.

My mother, who used her maiden name throughout her life, trained and worked as a teacher and was almost thirty when she met and married my father. She told me that she married late in life because, as the eldest child, she had to work to support her widowed mother and her six siblings.

On several occasions after her marriage my mother returned to teaching. In the small town where we lived in the Eastern Cape she took the initiative during the sixties to raise money to build an extra classroom, because the two-room school-house could no longer accommodate the expanding coloured community. She wrote short stories in her spare time, none of which were submitted for publication. She had a quick, analytic mind and a natural talent for business, although she did not get the opportunity to explore this further until after my father had died in the mid-sixties.

At this time I was teaching in Zambia. My passport had been withdrawn by the South African Nationalist government and I was unable to return home. With hindsight, I believe that my mother's decision to move to Swaziland, where she purchased a property, was in order to provide me and my daughter with an alternative home, but by that time I had already decided on Canada.

At the age of fifty-five, when most people think of retirement, my mother embarked on a new chapter in her life, a courageous step, because I know from personal experience how difficult it is to start a new life at that age.

Apparently the previous owner of my mother's property had had plans to develop it, but had died before he was able to act on them. Foundations had already been laid for two structures, about two hundred metres apart. One of these was on a slightly elevated part of the property, overlooking the other, a larger foundation that was closer to the main road. There was also an underground structure suitable for storing fuel. My mother engaged a small construction company to complete the work on the buildings. The larger one was to be a shop and the other her living quarters. She contacted a petrol supplier in Manzini and negotiated to have a petrol pump erected on the storage tank. It was an ancient hand-cranked pump that I swear had to be the prototype of all petrol pumps. But my mother didn't seem to care as she put up the 'petrol for sale' sign on the gate. She often pumped petrol herself, chatting with customers who showed interest in her plans for the property, which included opening an eatery – an open-sided rondavel with tables and chairs.

By the time the shop was completed and stocked, my mother had had a second petrol pump installed. It too was hand-cranked because there was no electricity yet. Because the property was just off the main road, local villagers, farmers and motorists on their way to Stegi or to Mozambique began to call. Her clientele of regulars expanded and my mother – a woman on her own – soon became something of a curiosity.

For the first two years her living conditions were primitive. There was no running water or sanitation and while her cottage was being completed my mother slept on a small cot in the shop storeroom. The lavatory was a rickety old wooden structure with a seat over a pit. In the absence of running water, my mother drove into Manzini every few days to fill three jerry cans with water.

She soon discovered that the property was infested with black mambas. My mother's solution to the problem was to tackle the mamba scourge by burning them out of their nests. One of the labourers would stuff the snake holes with cloth soaked in paraffin or petrol and set it alight. The mambas would come slithering out of the holes while my mother waited, shotgun at the ready.

She had never before used a shotgun or, indeed, a firearm of any description. Without much fuss she taught herself to shoot, using bottles and cans as targets at the far end of the property. Her first experience with the shotgun was a near disaster. Although she had been warned about the recoil effect of the shotgun, I guess she didn't realise how dangerous it could be. Forgetting the advice she had been given, she levelled the butt against her shoulder and fired. She was knocked off balance and bruised her shoulder so badly that she had to wear her arm in a sling for three weeks, giving the mambas a respite. As soon as she was well enough, though, she was back to shooting them again. My mother built up the business and was planning the small eatery when I asked her to join me in Canada. A few years later she sold the trading station and, at the age of sixty-two, she once more embarked on a new journey.

She was one of the most adaptable people I have ever known. With only the money from the sale of the property in Swaziland – which wasn't much in those days – she wanted to establish another business in Canada and immediately started considering all sorts of possibilities. But it was a bad time. Oil prices had plummeted, interest rates were at an all-time high and the economy was in recession. So she decided to find a job in order to get a feel for business. A friend of mine offered her work as a sales clerk in his boutique, but by this time his business, too, was struggling to survive and eventually he had to close down. My mother then spent a year at home taking care of my daughter while I was at work.

Mom was well educated and well read, and able to hold a discussion on any topic. She was a vivacious, energetic and intelligent woman who loved to party and loved to be surrounded by people. Men adored her – women weren't always that keen, but when she did make friends with them, they were friends for life. Because she loved beautiful things and had such expensive tastes, I always thought she should have been born into the Hollywood set. Her passion for and interest in diamonds led to a job in a top-class jewellery store, where she was so good at selling that she was soon promoted to the position of assistant manager. After some years at the store, a friend persuaded her to move to Lake Louise where an art store required a manager. It was a seasonal position, which my mother preferred. For the next few years, she spent every spring and summer in Lake Louise, where she got to know many of the celebrities who visited the resort. She had accommodation in the staff quarters. Most of the staff were young men and women barely out of their teens who came to Lake Louise for the lucrative summer jobs. The kids loved my mother, who partied as hard as they did.

The cold weather at Lake Louise, however, began to take its toll on her and she developed rheumatoid arthritis. Realising that she could no longer work there, she finally retired at the age of seventy-four. She returned to Calgary where I had bought a house and she lived with me for several years.

Mom had an uncanny knack for recognising good deals and could pinpoint a good property and land deal when she saw one, but of course she did not have the resources to follow up on them. It was extremely difficult for my mother to be idle and when I told her that I was thinking of buying a restaurant, she was ecstatic.

With her encouragement I went ahead and bought the restaurant, giving up my teaching job to become a restaurateur. I had no experience of the business but, challenged by my mother, I forged ahead. My mother loved the restaurant and thrived on the attention as she flitted around as the hostess. I discovered, however, that the restaurant was all-consuming and soul destroying. It was a seven-day-a-week job and I became both physically and emotionally bankrupt. I sold out before I became financially bankrupt.

During this time my mother met a wonderful man. At the age of seventy-eight she was about to get married again. A year later her partner died of complications from prostate cancer.

My mother hated being alone and two years after her partner died and I had moved to Vancouver, she met the love of her life at the age of eighty-two. The first two men in her life were both kind, considerate and loving, but in this man she found something special. He was three years older than she, and he died at the age of ninety-two in 1999. His death left my mother devastated and this was the beginning of her downhill spiral into depression and deteriorating health. She died on 26 February 2007 at the age of ninety-four.

I regret now that I had kept my mother at arm's length for so many years, but she was such a strong individual, with such a powerful presence, that she overwhelmed me. She was a forthright, independent-minded woman with strong opinions and could often be quite dominating. On many occasions I found myself in conflict with her as I fought to protect my individuality. Despite this, my mother was a very generous woman who always gave to those less fortunate than herself and, above all, she was always there when I needed her and for that I will always be grateful.

Those who met or knew my mother remember her as a 'character' with lots of spunk and attitude. Looking back now I regret that my relationship with her was not as warm and as close as it might have been if both of us had accepted, respected and appreciated our differences in the early years. I regret, too, that I did not spend more time with her. I often think of her now that she's gone and I do miss her terribly. At least we were close the last few years. I miss her wisdom, her sense of fun and humour on her better days when she was not in pain or in an antidepressant fog. I miss her easy laughter, her little expressions. One in particular comes to mind, which she had used in the year before her death. As if sensing what lay ahead, she used to say, 'I'm coming back to "ghost" you,' and I would laugh at the way she turned a noun into a verb. But that was my mother. She said that at her age she had earned the right to speak her mind.

I am sorry that I wasted so much time being angry with her for some of the issues that we never resolved, and that for many years there was no room in my heart for her. There is so much I want to say to her, so much that I want to tell her and thank her for – the strength and courage that I got from her and the way she taught me to be independent and committed to my principles – qualities that I in turn passed on to my daughter. I want to say all this to her but of course, it is too late now.

Farida Karodia, born in Aliwal North in the Eastern Cape, is a novelist and short-story writer. She taught in Johannesburg, Zambia and Swaziland in the sixties before the government of South Africa withdrew her passport in 1968. She emigrated to Canada where she published her first novel and did radio drama. After the end of apartheid, she returned to her home country.

Ahmed Kathrada

UNSUNG HEROES AND HEROINES

My mother, Howa, born and died in India

I never met my grandmothers, nor my grandfathers. They lived and died in India. As for my mother (and father), I have to blame apartheid for not really knowing them. I was born in a little rural town, Schweizer-Reneke, where there were schools for Africans and whites, but none for Indians. Therefore, at the age of eight, I was wrenched away from my parents and bundled off to school in Johannesburg, over two hundred kilometres away. Thereafter, I was schooled and grew to adulthood in Johannesburg. I only went home during school holidays. My father died when I was fourteen. My only memories of my parents are from my childhood years. They were very religious people; hence, there were some basic, indelible lessons that are ingrained since babyhood – respect for one's elders regardless of colour, etc.

Looking back now, there had been a number of women who played an important role in my life, some politically active, others not.

In Johannesburg, after leaving school, I renewed my association with the Pahad family, who also hailed from Schweizer-Reneke. In time, I came to regard Mrs Amina Pahad as my 'second mother', and was soon taken in as the eldest of her five sons. I knew her better than my biological mother. I have written about my attachment and love for her. In my *Memoirs*, published in 2004, I have written about her as a mother and politician. I also came to know other women who, like Mrs Pahad, were imprisoned in the 1946 Passive Resistance Campaign and in the 1952 Defiance Campaign. This was in addition to their other activities. Incidentally, two sons of my 'second mother', Essop and Aziz Pahad, are in the Cabinet today.

Then there were mothers of my friends and comrades, who, though not politically active, came to play a significant role in my life, especially in my pre-prison years. I've written about them as my 'Fordsburg aunts'. They were Mrs Vassen, Mrs Pillay and Mrs Reddi.

My biological parents were apolitical. When I was sentenced to life imprisonment, my brothers decided not to tell my mom for some time.

The family (including myself) also discouraged her from visiting me in prison because she was weak and we feared for what could happen to her.

My mother died while I was in prison. Because we were severely restricted in what we were allowed to write in our prison letters, I had to leave quite a bit out. For instance, I applied to attend her funeral and, not surprisingly, was refused.

This is an extract from a letter I wrote from Robben Island on 26 March 1972, on learning of my mother's death:

Dear folks …

… Thanks to Zohra, the shock of the news was not so great.

Nevertheless it is not possible to condition oneself fully for death. Deep in the recesses of the mind there always flickers a hope that somehow this spectre will be kept away from one's near and dear ones. One has reasoned and conditioned oneself that one day it has to come; yet when the blow strikes, the faculties are numbed and one reacts with all the emotion that is normal to human beings.

Of all our family I have spent the least time with Ma. In 1938, when I was just a little over 8 years old, I left home to attend school in Johannesburg. Until about 1946 I used to spend the school holidays at home. Some of you will recall the earlier years how unsuccessfully I used to hide my feelings each time I had to return to Johannesburg after the holidays. Mine must have been the normal reaction of a child who is wrenched away from its parents at so tender an age in order to attend school over 200 miles away. From 1946 my visits became shorter and less frequent. Then came my accident, the overseas trip, the return, the arrests, court cases, police raids, bannings, house arrest. I'm sure each of these must have caused Ma tremendous anxiety and sorrow. I'll never forget how she collapsed that day in June 1961 when I was brought home under escort on my way to Christiana jail. How happy she was for the few months in 1962 when I was free from bans and came home a good few times. But alas, the respite was too short. In October came the house arrest; a few months later I disappeared from home, and then came the Rivonia arrests, which ended in life sentences. I last saw her about 10 years ago. In jail I often reflected over the fact that I have been a constant source of worry and trouble to Ma and to all of you. I have lived with a slight feeling of guilt and have thought of ways and means of making good, but now Ma has been removed from us and I've been deprived of the opportunity. I do, however, find some consolation from the fact that all of you, more particularly her many grandchildren, and now the great grandchildren, more than made up for my absence.

… All my colleagues here, especially Mr Mandela and Mr Sisulu have asked to convey their deepest sympathy.

I recall the last time I saw my mother outside prison. In November 1962 she waited in the car downstairs in the street where I had a flat. Because my house arrest order prohibited any visitors (including my mother) from visiting me, I took a chance, broke my bans and went down to the car to greet her. My sister was also in the car with her new-born baby. I at least saw my sister when she visited me on Robben Island, and for some years after my release, before she died.

In 1992 I managed to carry out my mother's wish that I should undertake the Haj pilgrimage to Mecca on her behalf.

My mother's other wish was to see me married so I could present her with additional grandchildren. That was my desire as well when I was in my twenties. The love for children and the enjoyment of their company is a universal phenomenon. But our collective wish came to naught, and I was entirely to be blamed. All my family members, from my mother downwards, were greatly disappointed, embarrassed and angry with me. In retrospect, and with the advantage of maturity, I was able to ascribe my behaviour to youthful conceit – to an exaggerated idea of self-importance. I believed that marriage would interfere with my political activities!

I was thoroughly ashamed of myself and I cannot claim that I have freed myself of the feeling of guilt.

I never expected that my conceited and irresponsible behaviour would come back and haunt me in prison. Every prisoner would agree that of all the numerous deprivations of prison life the very worst would be the absence of children. I wonder if people outside prison believe me when I say that I had not seen, nor touched or cuddled a child for twenty years!

Yes, twenty years!

It happened in 1983, when my lawyer Ramesh Vassen came to see me in Pollsmoor prison. His three-year old Priya would not remain in the car. It was a touch of humanity and empathy that influenced the warder to relent. And for forty-five minutes or more little Priya sat on my lap, while I kept stroking her long hair. I was no longer part of the legal consultation. I was in another world, completely overwhelmed by a hundred emotions – love, compassion, joy, tenderness, beauty… It was an unforgettable thrill.

Not having carried out my mother's wish, I longed to claim Priya as my own and that feeling was repeatedly felt several times when children (and babies) were legally allowed to visit me. As they grew up, these bonds became stronger. I sent them birthday cards and occasional letters from Pollsmoor. After my release I continued this practice and attended the weddings of three young ladies who I had mentally claimed as 'my babies'.

I'm now the proud godfather of a number of children.

Today, 3 September 2008, is a special day for me. It is the third birthday of my very favourite Mateo, who has settled in far-off Australia with his mother, Kim. (Without Kim's devoted involvement, my *Memoirs* may not have seen the light of day.) Few things have I enjoyed more than the month they spent with us in Cape Town during April of this year. I take great delight in regularly speaking to him on the phone and savouring his tiny voice calling me 'Mr Kaai' – his version of 'Mr K'.

A very happy birthday my dear, dear Mateo. We miss you and love you. From Mr Kaai and Babwa.

I hope I will be forgiven for going off on a tangent of sentimentality. I'm invariably gripped by such a feeling when seeing, touching and playing with kids.

Ahmed Mohamed Kathrada (nicknamed Kathy) is a politician and anti-apartheid activist. He was one of the Treason Trialists in 1956 and one of the Rivonia Trialists in 1964; at the trial he was sentenced to life imprisonment, spending over eighteen years in prison. After the unbanning of the ANC he became a member of Parliament and in 1994 was appointed political advisor to President Mandela. In June 1999 he left parliamentary politics. He served as the chairperson of the Robben Island Museum Council. Kathy passed away 28 March 2017 in Johannesburg.

Sibongile Khumalo

GRACEFUL, GRACIOUS, ELEGANT

Grace Nonhlupho Mngoma (née Mondlane),
born 20 December 1923 in Western Native
Township, died 15 August 1987 in Empangeni

Graceful. Gracious. Elegant. Those are the three words that always come to mind when I think of my mother.

The last-born child of six siblings, my mother saw her first days in Western Native Township, a mixed settlement north-west of Johannesburg.

She married Khabi Vivian Mngoma on 26 October 1948, and my brother Lindumuzi Lester and I were the offspring that came of that union.

Mama was such a beautiful soul, both inside and out. Fair of skin, medium-sized body, to me she was the symbol of elegance. Even though in her later years she suffered from ill health, she very rarely complained, unless we were particularly unkind and paid no attention to her. And that happened sometimes.

Her elegance manifested itself not only in her carriage and dress sense, and she was a stylish dresser, but also in the way she related to others.

I very rarely saw my mother angry. If something or someone really got to her, she would say, 'Fancy, you know so-and-so has just done this or said that.' Then we knew she was angry.

She could not handle bad driving. Bad drivers really got to her. Then you would hear her use foul language, and that was rare. 'Aargh, voetsek man!' she would say to an incorrigible road user. Then she was really, really angry. But then again she might have been freer with her friends, I don't know. But in my presence, Mama always carried herself with a great deal of elegance and decorum. 'Fancy' was her swear word of choice!

I learned from her how precious relationships with sister-friends are. It only began to make sense when I was a grownup, how important these were. She had about four or five very close female friends, and each one of them had a very special place in her heart. I could see by the way she related to them, by the way she made time for each one of them, how much they meant to her.

Even with my female friends Mama created individual and special relationships. My friends knew that my home was theirs too, and Mama was always there to welcome them, to take care of them. Sometimes this made me feel very jealous because it felt like I was being replaced.

Mama believed in etiquette and good manners. But then she was very typical of her generation in that way. You would not, could not, serve my mother tea or anything else on a tray without a tray cloth. She considered that to be very slovenly and uncaring. Not only was a tray supposed to be covered, but you had to warm the teapot and cup as well. Tea was always accompanied by cookies or cake or something. We would be asked, 'Why are you giving me a gargle?' if there was no accompaniment for the tea. I guess it was the influence of the English, I don't know.

How food was presented was very important to her. When we grew up, serving oneself was not a very common practice in most homes. Once the dinner was prepared, you then had to dish up for the household. You can imagine how much time that took. It did not matter how much homework you had to contend with either. Preparing dinner and dishing up and washing the supper dishes afterwards was one of the responsibilities of growing up. If you ducked and went to sleep, you could be woken up in the middle of the night, and that was not nice.

Anyway, I digress. Mama was very strict about how food was presented on a plate. I began to understand later that it was a statement of caring and empathy. If you cared, then you made sure that the food was presented in an elegant and appetising way. It could drive me nuts as a child, but I understood, when I was older and had children of my own, how that seemingly small act translated into something so important. I have seen how my brother, Lindumuzi, pays attention to how he prepares and presents food, at those rare moments when he does.

Mama sang in the community choir that my dad had founded in the early 1960s, the Ionian Music Society. She was one of the soloists in the choir. In another time she could easily have made a career as a singer. She had a rich contralto voice. Even though untrained, it had a resonant, bright quality. I have memories of her singing the Brahms *Alto Rhapsody* accompanied by the Ionian Male Choir at the Uncle Tom's Hall in Orlando West, Soweto.

I can hear her singing the alto solo part in Handel's *Messiah*, Mendelssohn's *Elijah* and other great oratorios that the choir presented. She had a compelling stage presence. In fact, at the start of my career, I would sometimes get freaked out by the sound I was making, because it reminded me so much of her.

Mama was a professionally trained nurse and healthcare worker. As a nurse she had what could be called 'healing hands'. It did not matter what ailed you and how basic the medication she gave you was. If it came from her, you could be healed, and people usually were. An aspirin coming from her hands gave enormous relief even to the most aggravating ailment.

She was an incredibly good listener, a trait that always came in very handy for my father. For instance, when he was the head of the Music Department at the University of Zululand and he had major differences of opinion with his seniors, my poor mother would be woken up in the middle of the night because Daddy had some idea or thought he needed to share. If she complained, he would apparently ask her, 'Manje ngikhulume nobani?' ('So who must I talk to?') She would good-naturedly wake up, sit up and listen to his musings.

I learnt from observing her about the importance of being a good lover and friend to your partner, and the power of forgiveness. Like most couples, they went through their fair share of problems, but somehow she rode them and life went on. There was a 'girl-like' quality in her when she was around my dad. And yet she was a lioness where we children were concerned. She ensured that we were always protected from the vicissitudes of their existence both as a couple and as cultural workers who were always exposed to the whims of the government of the day in the sixties and seventies. For instance, I never heard her quarrel with my dad, even when I was aware there was tension between them. It is something I remembered and came to appreciate as a young married woman.

She had an abiding love for children and always took in relatives' offspring if someone was in need. She firmly believed that no one was to go hungry or unsheltered if we had a plate of food or a bed to share.

Even if that meant we children had to share the bed and not her. For the longest time I did not get it, but now I sort of do. She lived and breathed *ubuntu bakhe* (her humanness). I wonder how she would be feeling about the non-caring and materialistic society that we seem to have degenerated into.

Sis Grace, as her friends affectionately called her, was a pillar of strength, clichéd as that might sound, both to her family and to the different groupings of people she interacted with. When I meet people who knew her those many years ago, Mama is always remembered with love and affection. Bless her soul, she remains our greatest stay, a spirit that is:

[A] shelter embracing us all
That perfect place reached by conscience divine
You come in my dreams
And show me the way
You're my guiding light
And my inspiration
My guardian angel
My mountain shade

It is your grace that has taught love serene
Elegant love, there's none to compare
Just as the rain soaks the earth
And feeds it too
Lush is your smile
And vast is your strength
It knows no bounds

You rejoice where there's love
Where there's light and forgiveness
Peace and serenity
Gracious host
Mountain shade

I seek for inspiration from above
[The] clouds change shape
And I see your face
You are always there for me

From the song 'Mountain Shade' – music by Moses Molelekwa and
lyrics by Sibongile Khumalo

Sibongile Khumalo was born and grew up in Soweto and later studied violin,
singing and history of music at the University of Zululand and the University
of the Witwatersrand. She is one of South Africa's great singers. She was
the first person to sing the title role of Princess Magogo in the first African
opera *Princess Magogo kaDinuzulu* and has established herself as both an
opera and jazz singer in South Africa and beyond.

Sihle Khumalo

WHIPS AND THUNDERSTORMS

Rebecca Duduzile 'Dolly' Sithole, born 24 April
1942 at Nkandla

As to be expected of a black South African, I did not inherit anything from either of my grandfathers. However, my maternal grandfather – who was a local chief of the Sithole clan at Qhudeni in deep-rural KwaZulu-Natal – left behind a phenomenon called my mother. Rebecca Duduzile Sithole – better known as 'Dolly' because, apparently, she looked like a Barbie doll when she was a toddler – is, even after my spending more than thirty years with her, still an enigma.

Out of all the recollections I have of my mother, there is a single one which I clearly remember as if it were yesterday: the way she use to punish me when I had done wrong. It's not so much that I was a naughty young boy; it's just that my mother had very simple but non-negotiable rules. One of them was: I must always be home before sunset. The biggest problem with that rule was that I used to take part in a soccer game that only ended once one team had scored four goals. Hence sometimes one game – depending on the drought of goals – could last a whole day. Now that was where my troubles began.

When I got home at dusk, she would talk to me as if there was nothing wrong. About an hour later, when I had even forgotten that I had broken one of the house's standing rules, she would take out a whip – which had been hidden under her arm all this time – and give me a very good hiding. Whilst whipping me, she would not only be talking to me but she would also be asking questions, like 'Didn't I tell you to come home before sunset?' or 'Why don't you listen to me?' Sometimes, if I cried longer than anticipated, she would whip me whilst asking the question: 'Why are you crying?' A few days later, due to the inability of strikers to score goals during the soccer match, I would come back after sunset and the same procedure would ensue.

This whipping thing continued until I was well into my teens. She never had it in her to treat me like a typical last-born, i.e. a spoilt mama's baby brat. Together with my sister – who was getting whipped now and then for leaving the dishes unwashed overnight – we made a plan to steal the whip and bury it in the garden. That would be the last time we got whipped; at least that is what we thought. She got another whip from a neighbour and we got whipped until we dug out the original one.

Besides the whipping, another thing that I remember clearly growing up is how scared she was – and still is – of thunderstorms. In fact, she was so terrified of lightning and thunder that at the beginning of every summer season a well-recommended traditional healer would come home to make us 'stronger' – *izosiqinisa* – so that, come rain or shine, no thunderbolt would ever land at home.

Over and above that, my mother – at the earliest sign of the gathering of dark clouds – would cover the mirrors, switch off the radio, instruct us not to sit on chairs but on the mat and also not to mention other people's names, just in case those people were witches. Once the lightning and thunder began, she would give all of us a small part of the root of a tree – left behind by the traditional healer – to keep under our tongues.

Due to the bitterness of this muti, the generation of saliva in the mouth would be extraordinary. Obviously we had no choice but to swallow that bitter saliva for as long as the thunderstorm persisted. Sometimes, especially if the thunder got heavier, she would smear us – in a shape of a cross – with a black, sticky, Vaseline-like concoction on our foreheads. As if that was not enough, every time there was a big bolt of lightning she would raise her hand and say – at the top of her voice – 'Shwele!' ('Mercy!')

I do not blame her, not at all. She was born and grew up within a polygamous family where her grandfather – uMatshane kaJobe Sithole – had thirty wives and, as expected in such big families, witchcraft accusations and counter-accusations would pop up now and then.

Although my maternal grandmother – one of the seven wives of the late Chief Manzekhofi kaMatshane kaJobe Sithole – could not read or write, she not only knew most of the Anglican Church hymns by heart but also had very strong African traditional beliefs. My mother is exactly like that: she mixes religion – specifically Christianity – and traditional beliefs with such ease you would think they are complementary. For instance, the way she would pray and also talk about having a personal relationship with God, you would be forgiven for thinking she sometimes has a cup of coffee with God. At the same time – at least once a year, especially after a dream of one of the deceased family members – she insists that we must slaughter a chicken, goat or cow and brew some sorghum beer. When I have questioned her about mixing Christianity and traditional beliefs, her classic response has always been 'UJesu angeke sim'bambe ngezandla' ('We will never be able to physically touch Jesus.')

As a single parent, and with no mature male figure to talk to the ancestors as it is practised in the African tradition just before the slaughtering of an animal, she consistently took it upon herself (and without fail) to tell our ancestors exactly what our dreams and aspirations were. Well, it seems like the ancestors listened to her, because all her children, with the exception of her only daughter, are – in black people's standards – very successful. They are graduates, married, have a car and own property in a 'white' suburb.

Against all odds, she managed not only to get a Junior Certificate (JC, as it was called at the time), but also a one-year teacher's diploma. Almost twenty years later, as expected of all qualified teachers at the time, she had to attain – through correspondence – a Senior Certificate (Standard Ten or Grade Twelve as it is called today). To say she struggled to get that certificate is an understatement. She failed for five consecutive years and eventually passed on her sixth attempt. Needless to say, we prayed and thanked God for His late, but well-appreciated intervention. Naturally, a few weeks later we slaughtered a goat and thanked the ancestors for delivering the Senior Certificate and thus an increase in her salary.

Throughout her teaching career, which spans more than forty years, she taught Sub A (Grade One). That consequently meant all three of her children, as well as her first grandchild, were taught by her in their first year at school. She ensured that kids were taught discipline by using the very same whip that she used at home. Every morning she literally carried the whip in her handbag from home to school and took it back with her in the afternoon.

If there is one thing that my mother used to tell us consistently – I mean religiously – it was: 'Ningajabulisi izitha' ('Do not make our enemies happy.')

I guess, again, that stems from growing up in a polygamist family. It was imperative – as a kid – not to set your foot wrong. As a result and thanks to her, I – and surely my brother and sister as well – grew up with this desire to be somebody, to make it in life and thus disappoint our enemies. I must confess, though, that now that I have grown up I am not so sure who these enemies are that I have to displease.

She single-handedly created a safe haven for us and ensured that, through her constant words of encouragement and unconditional love, we became the best we could be in life. One thing that she believed in – besides religion and African tradition – was, and still is, education. In retrospect I can see that she never really enjoyed her meagre salary because, to her, if there was one thing that she had to give us, it was proper education. In fact, she even used to say, 'When I die, there is nothing that I will leave behind for you, but with proper education, even when I am no more, you will be able to fend for yourself properly.'

Now that she is getting older and has retired, she is more talkative, although she subjectively believes that she only speaks when there is a need to. That explains why there is no dull moment when she is around.

As kids, my sister and I secretly called her *uRD* (her initials) and now that I am married, my wife and I secretly call her *iDQ* – the Drama Queen.

I, together with your two other children who – although educated – cannot write, would like to offer our whipping and thunderous appreciation. *Siyabonga kakhulu* – thank you very much, RD.

Sihle Khumalo was born in Nqutu, a small, rural town in northern KwaZulu-Natal. He is a Technikon Natal (now Durban University of Technology) and Wits Business School graduate. He is the author of *Dark Continent My Black Arse* (Umuzi, 2007), which covers his epic Cape to Cairo expedition. He currently lives in Johannesburg with his wife and daughter.

Antjie Krog

TWO 'USELESS' RECIPES FROM MY
MOTHER AND AN UNSENT LETTER

Susanna Jacoba Krog (née Serfontein), born
30 April 1925 in Kroonstad

1.

'My plant is dead,' I overheard my mother saying to my father. 'I'm going
to Ta' Maria in Parys to get another one.' Plant? Ta' Maria? Who on earth
was still being called Ta' Maria?

The 'plant' appeared to be my mother's bread yeast plant she got
from her mother, who got it in turn from her mother, and so forth, back
to the Anglo-Boer War – the origin of this plant. One uses the plant to
bake bread and *boerbeskuit* with nothing more than one spoon of sugar,
one spoon of salt, six spoons of fat and ten double hands of flour.

I went with my mother to Ta' Maria. She waited on a *bankie* next to
the kitchen backdoor of a small roughly plastered house, with two long
limpid grey braids and a fruit jar on her lap. My mother handed over a
bundle of notes and I remember noticing that Ta' Maria's feet looked like
two roughly plucked chickens.

The jar was quarter-full of 'plant'. From that very same plant comes
the one in my own and my sister's fruit jars. Yes, although it is the
twenty-first century with the biggest variety of breads and beskuit ever
in human history, I bake *boerbeskuit*.

The baking usually starts as follows: you notice the beskuit is finished. You think you will go and buy some.

You stand in the *tuisnywerheid* or in front of 'Ouma's Rusks' at the
supermarket and you remember your mother saying: 'Jong, a woman
who does not even bake her own beskuit …' – with the silence completing the sentence conveying possibilities ranging from treason to
fratricide to rotting fingernails.

So you sigh and go back home. You take the plant from the shelf,
add sugar, salt and lukewarm water. You clean the pans, you wait for the

yeast to rise, you make a second, bigger morass-like batch and wonder why you are doing it.

The main characteristic of *boerbeskuit* is that it is quite hard and un-soakable. 'You mean hard-ish,' my mother would sniff, 'but it had to withstand all kinds of weather in a leather *saalsak* while on commando. Your ancestors fought the whole war on this.'

And finally it is time to knead. Knead? 'How can a woman negotiate her own life if she can't knead properly?' my mother would ask. Yes, not pummelling against a hump of dough with skinny red fists, no, but bringing the fists down, slowly and purposefully right from your axils down into the dough as if to measure the real extent of your power. You feel how your fists become generous, with buttery strategy, in where they want to place themselves and how the texture of the dough changes under your knuckles. As you knead you feel how the heat rises blissfully towards your elbows.

You put a lid on the bowl and cover it with your bread blanket. 'People don't have bread blankets any more,' my mother would sigh, 'because nothing grows old in their houses any more – everything is either new or rubbish.'

By early afternoon the dough has risen and is pouting like a maiden's buttock from the bowl. You roll arms of dough, cut them with a knife, pack double layers into your bread pans and put them into the oven. After half and hour the smell starts to fill the kitchen. It drifts through the neighbourhood. It teaches people the word 'reeling'. It enables them to spell 'salivary glands'. Your family comes from their rooms and games and books and iPods to stand in the door openings. You boil water for coffee. Your neighbours will forgive you for anything if you invite them now.

When you turn the batch with its light brown bursting crests out onto the table everyone is ready with plates and butter, knives, apricot jam and marmite. You grate some cheese. Thick soft pieces disappear with burning fingers. 'People don't cook properly any more,' my mother would say. 'In these white kitchens, they only seem to mix cocktails or chop vegetables for the TV.' What is left is dried in the oven overnight.

Next time you think, 'This really takes too long,' and you bake a five-star recipe with 500 g margarine, two cups of sugar, a house payment of seeds and fruit, yoghurt and vitamins, a spade full of baking powder. And you become sick of it, sick! And then, next time … you take the fruit jar off the shelf …

2.

Wash the baby's head with pure soap (Pears). Lightly rub olive oil into the scalp to prevent cradle cap. Fill a *kommetjie* with boiled water. Add three drops of glycerine and borax to sterilise the water to clean eyes, nose and mouth. Swab the eyes softly with two pieces of cotton wool soaked in this water. Roll thin stems, wet them and clean the nose. Roll some cotton wool around your little finger, wet it with the sterilised water and gently clean the inside of the baby's mouth to prevent sprue.

Warning: do not coo and giggle into baby's face. (Imagine enormous nostrils and stained teeth; imagine terrible breath and germs.)

One drop of white spirits on the navel, cover it with a bandage after the dried chord has fallen off so that the navel settles nicely within the stomach. Use a few drops of sweet oil on the penis and stretch the foreskin gently after the bath. Do so regularly until the foreskin slips over the stem – about two weeks. Make a powder of one part boracic powder and three parts Maizena. Use liberally behind the ears, neck folds, the thighs and between the toes. Lanolin torch brand for nappy rash and Kamillosan ointment for sore nipples when breastfeeding.

Warning: don't anguish when kept awake – you're not writing an exam tomorrow.

3.

Wissenschaftskolleg
Berlin
6 November 2007

Dear Mother

I am filled with longing today, but find I cannot write: Dear Mother, if only you were with me at last night's lieder concert in the Staatsoper where they sung the different compositions based on Goethe's poems. Or even: Dear Mother, if only you could be my German teacher again and read to us in that dusty Kroonstad classroom with enormous clouds gathering far out over the plains: 'Kennst du das Land wo die Zitronen blühn' and your mouth strange, so utterly strange forming the words: 'Im dunkeln Laub die Goldorangen glühn,' the strong aspirated h sound in your throat: 'Die Myrtle still und hoch der Lorbeer steht?'

Here in Berlin where a 'mächtiges Hochdruckgebiet über Norden Russlands' will bring to 'Mitteleuropa kalt-trockenes Wetter mit Schneeflocken.' (God, everything sounds so much colder in *Deutsch*!) I suddenly remember the majestic thin-nosed face on the painting against your wall in the old-age home. You told me that it was a self-portrait made by a German painter while he was interned during the Second World War. It would have been his task after the war to make important-looking paintings of the new Afrikaner leaders who would then have been freed from British rule by a victorious Germany.

For a time he hid down by the river on your farm. Every second day you were sent on your horse to take him food and paint. When he was later caught and interned, he sent you this self-portrait, with one eye blue and one green, as well as a small painting of the river that now hangs in my house in Cape Town.

The letters in Gothic script in your bottom drawer, did he write them? The poems? Is this how your extensive German library, collected over many years in our godforsaken town, started? Is that why you studied German at university?

I don't know how to ask you how you bring together in your mind this beloved German, waiting in the veldt, and the Jewish record dealer in town, phoning to say that 'etwas neu' had arrived. And then you would go to his shop and he would play for you your first Schubert lieder, Schumann, Wagner, pointing out what to listen for. Sometimes he was moved, you said. What did he make of this seventeen-year-old Afrikaner girl who was his only client listening and buying German lieder? This we do not talk about, nor about the language in which the longings of both of these men, one in hope, one in despair, were lodged thousands of kilometres away from Germany.

Nor do I know what to make of the fact that on Christmas Eve I sat in the pews of the Grunewaldkirche with your son-in-law and grandson – hearing the well-known carols, sung in God's language, as you used to say. A few minutes before midnight there was time for silent prayer. The lights were switched off and the doors of the old church opened onto the snow. Then right across the city all the church bells started to peal. We held hands as we sat there, encapsulated in this enormous European pulse, but we were three Africans. We were from so far away, and yet, looking at us, nobody would guess. This broke my heart.

I cannot say to you in this letter that it was when you read 'es schwindelt mir, es brennt / Mein Eingeweide. Nur wer die Sehnsucht kennt / weiss, was ich leide' that something else, something *unbestimmt* entered your voice, something that made my body, as young as I was, turn ice cold, a sound that I never heard from you ever again, but am spending a lifetime, I think, finding its source for you.

Your daughter

Antjie Krog is a prominent poet, academic and writer. Born in Kroonstad in the Free State to an Afrikaner family of writers, she grew up on a farm, attending primary and secondary school in the area. She published her first book of verse at the age of seventeen. Since then she has published nine further volumes and reported on the Truth and Reconciliation Committee. In 1997 she worked as parliamentary editor for the SABC. In 2004 she joined the University of the Western Cape as extraordinary professor.

Michael Lapsley

DEPTH AND SIMPLICITY

Laura Grace Lapsley (née Davis), born 1917 in
Hawke's Bay, New Zealand

Dear Mother

It was good to speak to you on the phone again today when I was looking
for the phone number of your big sister May on her ninety-sixth birthday.
You were surprised to hear my voice, as we had spoken a few days before
on your sixty-eighth wedding anniversary.

In recent times, it has been so good that, even though you live on the
other side of the world in New Zealand, we can speak often on a clear
phone line that makes you seem only a few inches away.

When you were eighty-nine, I did wonder if you would make it to
your ninetieth – pretty amazing for someone who has had seven children
and also endured her own share of ill health. I was overjoyed that you
reached your ninetieth and that you were happy that you did. It seems
only the other day that you were telling us that you hoped you would
make it to the year 2000.

I wonder whether you have moments in our relationship which are
significant to you, that I don't recall, and vice versa.

Do you remember the time I came home to say that I had seen a shirt
in a shop window that had pictures of stamps on and how desperately
I needed that shirt? I know that there was never any spare money at
home, but somehow you found the money. Thank you.

I always loved the way you sometimes called me 'Joseph' as a term of
endearment. You once said that you were not sure what you found harder
to cope with – my brother in a bad mood or me in a good mood.

When we were growing up, I had my share of quarrels with my

brother, who is just a year older. When you told your mother she expressed disbelief that I was capable of impossible behaviour.

In the year before I left home and the country to study for the priesthood and join a religious community, we had become more like equals in some ways. We could talk together about a variety of topics. You and Dad never tried to influence us about our life choices but supported us in what we decided to do with our lives. I was seventeen when I left and since that time I have only come home for holidays.

I remember when you came to Australia with Dad for my ordination as a priest, my ordination being the fulfilment of a lifelong dream for you. I studied in Australia and since 1973 my whole life has been spent in the countries of southern Africa. As the years passed I found that you had begun to speak to me as a child. When I asked you why, you said very honestly that it was because you didn't know me any more, so it was easier to return to a mother–child relationship. I knew the comment was true, but I found it very painful. For a number of years I was not relaxed and did not relate easily when I visited. In recent years this has changed and the relationship has become open and relaxed once more.

Inevitably it was a deep shock to you when I was bombed in Zimbabwe in 1990 and lost an eye and both hands. I remember the first time we spoke on the phone a few days after the bombing. Your visits were wonderful, but I am sure very painful for you, after I had been transferred to an Australian hospital.

You told me that you had told someone else that I would not return to live in New Zealand or Australia because my life's work was in Africa. I felt that you understood and accepted the choices I have made.

Over the last few years, as your physical health has deteriorated, I have been asking you often how you are doing. Unfailingly you will tell me how you are doing – often saying that you are wearing out but always insisting that 'In myself I am fine; emotionally and spiritually I am a hundred percent.' I know it is true. You have said that you have no fear of death. I know it is true.

Thank you for the way you have loved me and each of your seven children unconditionally. This has given me deep emotional stability.

One of the greatest privileges I have had has been to celebrate Mass in your home and give you Communion. Most humbling have been the occasions you have asked me to be a priest to you.

I admire and sometimes envy you for the depth and simplicity of your faith in God and the way you live out the Christian Gospel.

A year ago, my close friend Ndukenhle, whom you also met, died of AIDS just before Christmas. I was greatly moved by your compassion and support for me in the midst of my grief.

I am often amazed that you retain an abiding interest in my own involvement with the healing of memories.

Thank you for being proud of me. I hope I will be worthy of that pride. Thank you for being my mother.

With my prayers
Much love
Michael

Father Alan Michael Lapsley, SSM, is an Anglican priest, member of the Society of the Sacred Mission and social justice activist. Born in New Zealand and trained as an Anglican priest in Australia, he came to South Africa in 1973. He was one of the first two employees of the Trauma Centre for Victims of Violence and Torture in Cape Town, which assisted the Truth and Reconciliation Commission. In 1998 he founded the Institute for Healing of Memories and has been its director ever since.

Winnie Madikizela-Mandela

A STRANGER AT HOME IS A FRIEND YOU DO NOT KNOW

My paternal grandma, Margaret Mahlongwe Seyini Madikizela, born around 1879 in Bizana

When I was asked to write a few words about my grandma, I realised with horror that the emptiness I sometimes feel in my moments of solitude is a result of how much I miss her! So much so that I wish for her to be alive for me to tell her how much I love her.

My grandma was the envy of the entire tribe, and to understand her you have to understand our culture. To my despair, she passed away when I was only 21 years old and newly married. She is remembered by the following sons and daughters, most of them with colonial names: My father Kokani Christopher Columbus, school teacher; Ntsizi Phillip, agriculturalist; Mpepa Silas, businessman; Lamginya Delihlazo, shop owner; Xam Douglas, miner and businessman; Peter, miner; Bungelwa (daughter), teacher; and Mpiyonke (daughter), a married woman.

Because my mother died early in my life, my grandma came to live with us in our household. Home was composed of plus-minus ten rondavels and two main T-shaped, four-roomed houses with corrugated-iron roofs. The homestead was home for about twenty children and ten adults. It was instilled in us that a child was brought up by the community. Heads of the community were invariably grandmothers, who wielded more power than biological parents.

Our grandmother was a tall woman with striking features. Her beauty was enhanced by the traditional face marks like those that adorned OR Tambo's face. The tip of her left small finger was cut at birth to mark her as heir to her family, so she told us. She therefore had natural authority, even over our father and all her siblings.

Grandma was very strong, very strict and authoritative, but extremely protective of all of us. There was no difference between her treatment of her biological grandchildren and that of the children from the village. Each one of us was given a specific task and we knew we had to do our best to impress Grandma so that we got the best meat portion at dinner. Grandma dished up the food even if she did not cook it, especially on meat days, when father had slaughtered a goat, sheep or pig. There was no butchery near our rural home, so the rest of the meat was given to the nearby families.

In the evening there would be this huge fireplace in the middle of the hut, which was also a kitchen. The young girls would gather around it on one side sitting on grass mats woven by Grandma. She was the village specialist in weaving these mats, together with baskets for storing fresh mealies from the mealie fields and grass brooms, etc. When maidens got married to faraway places, Grandma supplied each family with these as part of the bridal gifts. I have no recollection of any family paying. As young girls we fetched the special reeds for weaving from the riverside and carried them on our heads under Grandma's supervision.

Grandma was the first victim of the Pondoland uprising when the Pondos revolted against the National Party's land control. They refused to let the government re-zone the land, causing the homestead to be in one area and the mealie fields to be in another section. No white man was to touch ancestral land and disturb ancestral spirits.

We competed over cutting the reeds because the weight of the load was meant to please Grandma, as we were always in groups. The larger your load was, the better the prospect of praise from Grandma, who taught us to strive for perfection and good standing in the community.

Father was the school principal at our local primary school for as long as I could remember. But still, at home, Grandma taught us to jump up and stand at attention whenever Father walked in for a chat with his mother in the kitchen. We all had to leave the fireplace where we listened to great traditional stories, handed down from generation to generation. So we didn't like it much when Father came to the hut.

It was here where Grandma and other grandmas from the village would tell us about the traditional initiation of young girls, which we all underwent later when we reached the age and after which we were never the same. We were elevated to a higher level of spirituality, intro-spection and almost to a sacrosanct secret understanding of our God that included that quote from the Bible, 'I am because I am.' Grandma made us believe, which I still do to this day, that a stranger at home is a friend you do not know. She taught us that a family is a family of the tribe. Grandma was herself one of more than ten wives of Chief Mazingi

Madikizela. When we lived with Grandma, she was a widow, grandfather having died before I was born.

Grandma was in control of all her children's lives. The daughters-in-law had a hard time trying to please Grandma, who was a perfectionist and very strict. The Madikizelas were a large family that covered about thirty districts at the border between Natal and the Eastern Cape. We were divided by the great Mzamba River, from where one sees the beauty of our land in summer – the breathtaking, undulating plains and winding roads leading to Bizana, my home, forty kilometres from the Wild Coast. At primary school, everyone, from the principal to the grade zeros and the teachers, were all Madikizelas. Grandma told us that we were a very important family that had sacrificed a lot to be educators. She told us how Father refused to be a chief so that he could go to school, come back and teach the rest of the tribe. We should emulate him, she believed.

She also told us of the wonderful old days, how she had been the first woman in the village to wear shoes. She was the only one for whom Grandfather (who was reported to have been very wealthy in terms of animal stock and cornfields) had built a shop. She was forced to convert into wearing Christian clothes. The shoes she described were tennis shoes or sneakers. She was very proud of the fact that she manned this shop herself and was the first of the chief's wives to take charge of her life and control over her children. This taught her that the power of women was greater than that of men.

As a result she was in complete control of our lives and that of our father. Father had married a beauty from the Mzaidumes, a Radebe family from the Hlubi tribe. The tribal description is not meant to be ethnic; it is, in relation to the traditional exchange and interaction, more anthropological and sociological, for the maintenance of the nucleus of the family. The effect of this was that a child belonged to the tribe, thus a child had to observe the norms, mores and discipline of the larger extended family. If you misbehaved you didn't face the wrath of Grandma only but that of the tribe.

Mother was very light complexioned, rather tall, slender and reserved. She was a Domestic Science teacher. She didn't wear the traditional black doek on her head. She made her own fashionable crochet hats and did not wear the then long German print fabric dresses, worn by every young *makoti* (newly-wed), and only changed on Sundays for church. Grandma hated the fact that Mother was light complexioned. She said Mother reminded her of the whites, the people who took her shop and persecuted her husband, a chief who had more authority over his tribe than them.

We listened to fireside stories from Grandma about how people who had silky hair, pale skins and blue eyes came into our land, challenged the big chief, her husband (who had never been challenged by his tribe) and stole her shop. She called these people 'Abanyepi' – meaning 'those who had toilets inside the house'. In those days all my grandmother knew was the outside pit because huts had no running water. Tragically, to this day people still do not have toilets inside the house in rural South Africa.

When she told us these stories, she would be lying prostrate on her stomach next to the door on a grass mat with a traditional wooden pillow, keeping a stick by her side. She was a heavy woman, like a chief's wife of old, and she could not run after us when we were naughty. Chiefs' wives had to be cushioned. Added flesh was the sign of a wealthy chief. No chief could afford to have a thin wife or he would suffer from village gossip. She knew that we had to enter or leave the common kitchen or 'sitting room' through that door. If you had been naughty and (in most instances) had forgotten about it, you would feel a sting on your ankle as her stick went to action, never missing, no matter how high you jumped.

We learnt never to forget our responsibilities. That is how she instilled in me complete independence and loyalty to whatever cause I support. She taught us never to approach Father for anything. She actually pro-tected Father from us and often mumbled that we should never worry her son, who worked very hard in the fields and taught at our school during working hours. She was a pensioner and kept her pension in what we as kids referred to as 'Grandmother's dairy' – her breast! She would tie it into a cloth and never took it out when she went to bed on her grass mat.

She often went to the village of Bizana to buy clothes for my father. She said we were grandchildren of those people who took her shop because of Mother's complexion, but she loved us dearly. She prepared our meal of *amasi* (very rich sour milk) on crushed, boiled mealies. This delicacy was called *umvubo* and was prepared in big dishes. Children ate together, and we would be a group of five or more. Grandma taught us that a respectable family shares whatever they have. There was a standing rule that we cooked for strangers who passed by, whether they had come to visit or not.

Her daughters-in-law were terrified of their mother-in-law, who was over-protective of all her children. We witnessed many sessions Grandma had with her daughters-in-law. We would eavesdrop. The women would emerge from the main hut wiping their eyes. Grandma never sided with them. She would reprimand them and tell them to leave her sons alone, as they had worked very hard for their wealth. As a result, all her sons were self-reliant and had different skills, mostly discovered after their marriage because of Grandma who was in charge of the economics of their households. She believed her daughters-in-law wanted her sons' wealth. But we as children loved our aunts and thought Grandma was wrong.

My father ran a little country shop next to the school. And just as easily he would run this shop to the ground each month! It was a little depot where all the pensioners cashed their bit of money and always exceeded their allowances buying groceries. Father never made a cent from the shop and Grandma often closed it, only to re-open it again later. Little did she realise that Father was running an unregistered welfare NGO in order to send me to Jan Hofmeyer School of Social Work to obtain my first diploma in Social Work.

Grandma would hold *imbizos* (family meetings) where she lamented the loss of their traditional land. To her, that part of Eastern Pondoland was invaded by those strange people who 'gave her children strange names that she could not pronounce and never did' and who preached on Sundays. Grandma knew that Pondoland would never be the same again. My father ended up being 'Khalembizeni', Grandma's translation of Columbus!

My mother's full names were Nomathamsanqa Gertrude Mzaidume 'MaRadebe'. The only thing grandma loved about her was that she gave her six granddaughters and four grandsons. After Mother had died, Father waited for all of us to finish high school before he remarried, but that was not enough for Grandma. My poor step-mom experienced hell from Grandma and we often defended her, to Grandma's annoyance!

Grandma was such fun! That was my grandma!

Winnie Madikizela-Mandela was born in Bizana. She became a politician and a well-known female leader in South Africa's history and is often referred to as the 'Mother of the Nation'. She has held several government positions, headed the ANC's Women's League and is currently a member of the ANC's National Executive Committee. She is the ex-wife of former president Nelson Mandela.

Mac Maharaj

'I CAN WRITE MY NAME!'

Suminthra Maharaj (née Singh), born
10 February 1907 in Bethlehem, died 27
August 1983 in Newcastle

Her tiny frame exuded energy and purpose. Her small strides had the quickness of knowing where she was going and the urgency of knowing why she was going there.

The sharpness in her features and firmness in her jawline were softened by the olive skin that bore not even the faintest traces of age. Her hands told a different story. The fingers were prematurely gnarled, the back of her hands wrinkled like a ripe granadilla skin, her palms scoured with lines.

She was always the first to rise and the last to rest. The larger routine of her day followed a narrow path that ran between the backyard, defined by a heap of coal and wood, a garden patch, a chicken run, through the kitchen, whose centrepiece was a coal-fired stove, to the general dealer's shop at the front of the house.

She traversed that path each day, criss-crossing a thousand times – shovelling coal, tending to the pots, cleaning the house, mending torn socks and trousers, sewing outfits for the family, serving customers in the shop, serving endless cups of tea for our chair-bound dad and his cronies gathered to talk about village and world events and to dwell on the grandeur of life and the inequities of the white man.

In the small routine of the day little was predictable. She responded to events and people on demand, knowing only that by the end of the day all had to be done and everyone's needs met.

Somehow within the uncertainties of this perpetual activity, there would descend a mid-morning quietness. In that still moment she would snatch the opportunity to bathe. Against the frame of her four feet eight inches, her hair in all its resplendent grandeur would reach the ground. She would bask in the backyard sun. The smell of coconut oil would fill the still air as she massaged her scalp and oiled her hair. It was her stolen moment of indulgence.

She would invite me to brush and plait her hair. She wore her hair in a single plait, twirled into a bun pinned at the crown of her head. I would secretly tease it into two plaits and tie them together at the end. She would react with surprise. Amid annoyance and laughter I would redo the plait. It was our time of bonding, of living in a bubble warmed by the gentle sun, perfumed with the pungency of coconut oil and far, far away from the bustle of things done and things to do – of that secret time when a gentle slap from her was the mark of a loving caress. It was our moment of tenderness, mischief and laughter sparkling in the glint of the sunlight.

She bequeathed to me an abiding sense of the difference between the educated, the lettered and the cultured.

She had never set foot in a school. Her children taught her to write her name in the English alphabet. Each time she completed that laboured scrawl she would proudly proclaim, 'I can write my name!'

When we acquired the shop she marvelled that Dad could write on a sheet of paper taken from a cheque book and voila! a debt was wiped off. She never could figure out the relationship between the act of depositing the earnings in a bank and the payment of a debt by writing a cheque. They were two discrete and unrelated events that took place at different times and in different spaces. Every time Dad fretted about the lack of funds and grumbled about the debts we owed she would gently remind him that he could make it all go away by writing out a cheque.

But she understood the cycle of the seasons and of life. She ferreted out the edible wild herbs in the veld, bandaged with splints the broken leg of a chicken, tended to our bruised limbs and hearts and served everyone with unfailing courtesy and recognition of their dignity. She knew when to plant and when to harvest. She knew that out of what was harvested some should feed us and some should be kept as seed for the next season.

Every birth – of seasons, plants, animals and humans – was a celebration. Every passing, the promise of a new life and an act of fate. Within the circle of life and death there was an inner core of reverence for all things living and for things to come.

She acknowledged and respectfully bowed to patriarchy while subverting it at every possible turn. Dad's orders went in one ear and passed out the other while she in her subversive and innocent way did what she thought right and proper. It was proper to listen to him and right to do what she thought was the right thing to do! She was like a stream of water that sought out the curvature of the landscape and carved out a pathway much like the meandering streams and cascading rivers of our beautiful land.

If she had had the good fortune to be educated – say to have become a nuclear physicist – would she have risen to the challenge of developing nuclear power? I think she would have. Would she have been beset with moral and ethical dilemmas because of the awesome power of nuclear fission and fusion? I think so. Would she have colluded with the development of the atom bomb? Maybe. Would she have colluded with the bombing of Hiroshima and Nagasaki? I think not. Would she have remained silent at the tens of thousands of civilians killed and future life maimed? No, she would not have.

She grew up on a farm. All her life she lived off the land. She was nurtured in a patriarchal system. Everything shaped her to be a conservative, to cling to the certainties of the present, to hanker after the past and fear the future and change.

But she learned to live with change. While she could make no sense of what I wanted from life, she encouraged me to search and find what I wanted.

4 February 2008
Johannesburg

Mac Maharaj served as activist and leader in the freedom struggle from 1953 until his retirement in 1999. He smuggled out from Robben Island prison the manuscript of what became the core of Nelson Mandela's autobiography *Long Walk to Freedom*. He edited and published *Reflections in Prison* in 2001 (Zebra Press). His biography, *Shades of Difference: Mac Maharaj and the Struggle for South Africa* by Padraig O'Malley, was published by Penguin, NY, in 2007. His wife, Zarina Maharaj, published her memoirs *Dancing to a Different Rhythm* in 2006 (Zebra Press).

Miriam Makeba

UNCONDITIONAL LOVE

Nomkomndelo Christina Makeba (née Jele), born in Swaziland, died August 1960

My mother, Nomkomndelo Christina Makeba, was born some time during the Anglo-Boer War. No one knows the exact birth date except that it was on the day that her father was commandeered into the British army, hence the name Nomkomndelo.

The bond that we had was very strong. I doubt this had anything to do with the fact that I am the last-born in my family. The story is that she had a difficult pregnancy with me. She almost lost her life, as did I. But thank goodness we both survived this – I otherwise would not have known her, let alone have experienced her love.

She was a phenomenal woman. I always remember her positive energy. She worked magic with her hands. She could bake as well as do lovely embroidery. She sang beautifully and danced as though she were gliding on clouds. I guess it is fair to say that music really runs in my blood.

From a very young age I learned the importance of hard work just from watching my mother. I got up at five in the morning to do my chores. These included sweeping the yard and fetching water from the well. I am still like this to this day. I find it difficult to just sit idly. Although I have gotten along in age, I love to cook for family and friends and run my own errands. I get up early in the morning and help my great-granddaughter prepare for pre-school. It does not matter to me that she has a nanny. I do it out of love.

I owe my success to my mother, without question. Through her encouragement I pursued a career in music. This was at a time when women in the industry were frowned upon, thought to be of loose morals. She said it was what my father would have wanted me to do. As a result I persisted and went on to do all that I had wished to do and to be more than just a musician.

I always knew how to make her laugh, especially when she was not feeling too good. I loved it when that happened. She was such a giving person that I never wanted to see her sad, ever. Making her laugh was the least I could do.

Although she passed away in 1960, she is still a very real part of my life. Her leaving the physical world was very sad for me and my family. I was unable to attend her funeral because I was in exile and one of the first things I did when I was allowed to come back home was to visit her grave.

I see her in everything I do. I am where I am today because I worked hard. I also believe that the kindness and blessings of my ancestors play a part, especially my mother whom I believe is always smiling down at me.

Being a mother and grandmother myself, I can only but try to do the same for my grandchildren and great-grandchildren – love them unconditionally and support them in what they choose to do for themselves.

Miriam Zenzi Makeba, also known as Mama Afrika, was a world-renowned singer and civil rights activist. She was born in Johannesburg to a Swazi mother, who was a sangoma, and a Xhosa father, who died when she was six. Her professional career began in the 1950s. She left South Africa to live in the States and in Guinea. In 1966, she received the Grammy Award for Best Folk Recording together with Harry Belafonte. She only returned to South Africa after Nelson Mandela persuaded her to come home in 1990. She died in Italy on 10 November 2008.

Rian Malan

SOME THOUGHTS ABOUT
MY MOTHER

Dorothea Allan, 'Vi', Malan (née Gay), born
19 March 1924 in Johannesburg

I would rather not be writing this, and I struggle to understand why. Is there a taboo lurking hereabouts? Some dark Freudian monster whose existence I've never acknowledged, let alone confronted? It seems un-likely, because such things didn't exist in our world. We lived in a bright new suburb on the outskirts of a big city. We subscribed to *Reader's Digest* and *Huisgenoot* and the prim white middle-class values they upheld. We were solid people. We went to church on Sunday. Our granny was full of Victorian aphorisms like 'Procrastination is the thief of time,' or, 'The devil makes work for idle hands.' We did not use four-letter words, especially not the one beginning with L. One might say 'I'd love a cup of tea.' But one did not say 'I love you.'

Which is not at all to say that our lives were devoid of love. We loved our dogs, we loved the sentimental Italian tenor Mario Lanza and, above all, we loved our servant Lena, a radiant Zulu woman who had a red-bead wig and a fly whisk and a parallel life as a sangoma of great standing. On Thursdays, maid's day off in the suburbs, a knot of clients would materialise at our garden gate, awaiting admission to Lena's consulting room. My mother loved those people too. She didn't like tsotsis, but she had a soft spot for people we called 'natives' – especially the 'raw' or 'good' ones who called her 'Madam' and took off their hats when they asked to come inside. She would give them tea with three spoons of sugar and ask where they came from. In those days, natives were always 'from' somewhere, usually some forlorn tribal homeland through which we drove on our way to Christmas holidays at the sea.

The natives always smiled and waved at us, and my mother insisted that we smile and wave back. So it is easy for me to say I grew up loving natives. It is the other thing that is more difficult.

In one of my earliest memories, it is a preternaturally bright and cold day on the Highveld. The sun is shining, but the cold inside our house is so bitter that my mother and I have gone to bed in mid-morning, and she is singing a haunting lullaby to me, some heartbreaking song about a ship sailing out across the bar, carrying a sailor who will never come back again. I said, 'Sing it again.' She did. And again. And again. We lay there all morning, singing that sad song, and the memory of it is like an ache in my chest. But we did not say we loved each other. We were just not that kind of people.

Did I mention that my mother was beautiful? And clever? She skipped several classes at school and matriculated at sixteen. After that she went to Cape Town, and by the age of nineteen she was a teacher. She was also English, born into a clan that worshipped the Royal family and observed the essential British rituals of tea, straight bats and stiff upper lips. Their sons – educated, of course, at colonial sub-Etons called Saint this or King's that – considered it a privilege to fight and die for the Empire. They did it in 1899 and again in 1914 and 1939. There was no doubt in their minds that Britain was the source of all things worthy and superior, and that Afrikaners were uncouth and backward. I doubt that my mother had ever met one socially until she met my father, the enemy.

And he really was the enemy, my old man. The year was 1943, and he was a hard-line Afrikaner nationalist who'd walk out of the bioscope in protest if they played 'God Save the King'. He was a member of the virulently anti-British and semi-clandestine Ossewa Brandwag. She favoured a movement called Sons of England. His whole being was dedicated to ousting the British imperialists; she turned out to squeal and wave flags during Royal Tours. My mother's friends were horrified when she agreed to a date, and then another, and another …

Such love affairs were deemed 'interracial' in newspapers of the period and frowned on by both sides. My mother was denounced by her other suitor, a Royal Air Force pilot with handlebar moustache. The family began to ostracise her. The headmistress of the rather posh English girls' school where she taught gym hauled her onto the carpet and ordered her to drop the Afrikaner on the grounds that dating him just wasn't the done thing. As for the old man, he was cornered by his comrades from the nationalist movement and bullied to tears for his betrayal.

In the end, social pressure was such that they parted, but something odd happened a year later. My father was a shy and fundamentally decent man, seldom given to displays of emotion. He said nothing when his English rose left town, and uttered no rebuke when he heard she was planning to marry a gentleman farmer in the Eastern Cape. But on the day her train passed through Queenstown, he got on his bicycle and, driven by a force whose name we did not speak, rode to the station, where he fell to his knees and begged her to reconsider. She got off the train, and that was that.

As a boy, I had no inkling that my parents were capable of such passion. I thought my mother was like all other mothers, only prettier, but perhaps I am wrong here. Do other mothers sing and dance while cooking macaroni cheese for supper? Do they talk to dogs and small boys as equals? Do they give visiting natives tea and quiz them in Fanagalo about their putative mud huts and cattle? Do they teach in 'special schools' and bring Salvation Army orphans home for weekends? One of those waifs was Dennis Owen, and he was handicapped, so he had no problem telling my mother that he loved her. He wrote to her for years, for decades. His letters were childlike and barely legible, but there was no mistaking their message: he loved her.

Dennis was sweet and dog-like in his devotion. It was an example I should have profited from, but I grew up to be a snotty little punk interested largely in long hair, rock music and myself. By the age of sixteen I'd taken to calling my mother 'Sarge', in recognition of her generally fruitless efforts to get me to shape up and make something of myself. By the age of twenty-two I'd left the country, styling myself as a Just White Man too noble to bear weapons for apartheid. My mother bore it stoically because she had problems with apartheid too. She was anything but a liberal, but she did believe one should be kind and fair to everyone. Towards this end she squabbled with my father and voted for the United Party, which stood for a kinder, gentler and English-speaking variant of white domination.

Revolution was of course unthinkable. By the time I returned to South Africa in the mid-eighties, the struggle was underway in earnest and my mother, like most whites, was growing a bit gatvol. She'd say things like, 'They want everything on a plate,' or, 'What did they do to build this country? They just dug where we said dig.' In recent years, she developed a major grievance about the changing accents of the announcers on the English radio service of the SABC and, after the debacle in Zimbabwe, took to denouncing President Mugabe and all who protected him as barbarians. But she never quite rid herself of the habit of being nice to natives.

Consider this: it's a Friday afternoon in a small Free State town, and my mother is setting up a table at the gate of the retirement village where she lives in widowhood. She's been retired for decades, but still gets up at six and spends her days working. She runs the village library, organises bingo games, campaigns for the Democratic Alliance and agitates for pay rises for security and nursing staff. She also manages the complex's tuck shop, in which capacity she extends credit and small loans to men she still refers to as boys, as in 'garden boys' or 'the builders' boys'. This tiny philanthropy is viewed as madness by her septuagenarian neighbours. They say, 'Ag, you'll never get your money back,' but she always does. Come payday, she sits at the gate with her ledger, a tiny and frail creature picking out faces in the passing stream and hectoring them to come pay their five rand. Outsiders would find it quaintly patronising, but I don't know. The labourers are hugely amused by her Fanagalo and old-fashioned ways. There is lots of laughter, and if anyone is really strapped, she always says, 'Next week, okay?' The neighbours think it's just a matter of time before she gets robbed, but I could almost swear those men love her.

Is this sounding like a hagiography? If so, I must retract. My mother was capable of unbearable sweetness, but she had a very strict side too. My first school reader was a picture book that told the story of a horse called Dobbin, as I recollect. Within weeks, I could reel off Dobbin's adventures from start to finish, but I wasn't really reading; the pictures triggered associations, and I was reciting by rote. When she realised this, my mother made a mask out of a sheet of newspaper, blotting out the pictures and forcing me to focus on the hieroglyphs beneath. I threw a tantrum; she whipped me with a fly swatter. I ran outside, thinking dire thoughts of vengeance and muttering 'Bloody Mommy'. I remember this because I thought God had surely heard me and that I would be struck dead for such a sin. But the medicine worked, and I learnt to read.

Strictness aside, my mother's greatest vice was loving indiscriminately. My father used to say, 'Daar's dinge wat jy lewenslank saamsleep' – 'There are things that you carry with you forever.' Muttering 'Bloody Mommy' is not one, but there are others. The embarrassment caused by my sometimes wild behaviour. All the letters I never wrote when I lived on the far side of the planet. The way I treated her when she came to visit me in America after nearly a decade away from home. I was a *windgat* investigative reporter onto a hot story. My absurd ambitions took precedence. She sat in a hotel for two days until I found time to see her. It must have caused terrible pain, but she just smiled. She is like that.

The other day I took a friend to visit her. The friend is an artist, a militant feminist with tattoos on her shoulder, a bevy of proudly illegitimate children and some very strange ideas about the human spirit. My mother is eighty-four, and very straight. I assumed our tea party would be extremely awkward, but I underestimated my mother. They talked for hours, going deep into reaches of the heart where I dread to tread. I listened in silence, staggered by my mother's ability to draw people out and by the wisdom emerging from her lips. I was thinking how extraordinary she was, and how deeply I loved her. I was thinking how good it would be, just once, to talk to her as the stranger did. But I wouldn't know where to begin, and besides, people like us don't go there. We just call for another cup of tea.

Rian Malan was born in Johannesburg and is an author, journalist and songwriter. To avoid forced military enrolment he moved to the USA where he became a writer and keen observer of the violence in contemporary society. He returned to South Africa in the eighties and wrote *My Traitor's Heart*, a memoir about growing up in apartheid South Africa.

Nelson Mandela

'UQINIS' UFOKOTO, KWEDINI!' ('BRACE YOURSELF, MY BOY!')

Nosekeni Fanny Mandela, died 24 September 1968 in the district of Umtata, presumed age 74 years

I was born on 18 July 1918 at Mvezo, a tiny village on the banks of Mbashe River in the District of Umtata, the capital of the Transkei ... My father Gadla Henry Mphakanyiswa was a chief by both blood and custom. He was confirmed as chief of Mvezo by the king of the Thembu tribe ... The Thembu tribe reaches back for twenty generations to King Zwide. According to tradition, the Thembu people lived in the foothills of the Drakensberg mountains and migrated towards the coast in the sixteenth century, where they were incorporated into the Xhosa nation.

Xhosa society was a balanced and harmonious social order in which every individual knew his or her place. Each Xhosa belongs to a clan that traces its descent back to a specific forefather. I am a member of the Madiba clan, named after a Thembu chief who ruled in the Transkei in the eighteenth century. ... Ngubengcuka, one of the greatest monarchs, who united the Thembu tribe, died in 1832. As was the custom, he had wives from the principal royal houses: The Great House, from which the heir is selected, the Right Hand House, and the Ixhiba, a minor house that is referred to by some as the Left Hand House. It was the task of the sons of the Ixhiba or Left Hand House to settle royal disputes ... The eldest son of the Ixhiba House was Simakade, whose younger brother was Mandela, my grandfather.

*

Mandela was the son of a Pondo Princess. And then the mother of Mandela the princess ruled the southern part of Thembuland. ...We have women, we have had women, in Thembuland taking leading positions, ruling the country and the mother of Mandela was such a person. ...

Because the mother of Mandela, when the English came to our area, she decided to fight them. She came from the Pondo house of Sigcau and so the English when they defeated her deported her back to Pondoland. But at least she had the distinction of mobilising the Thembu to fight against the whites. And that's why they deported her back to her home where she came from.

*

All told, my father had four wives, the third of whom, my mother, Nosekeni Fanny, the daughter of Nkedama from the amaMpemvu clan of the Xhosa belonged to the Right Hand House. Each of these wives – the Great Wife, the Right Hand Wife (my mother), the Left Hand Wife and the wife of the Iqadi or support house – had her own kraal. A kraal was a homestead and usually included a simple fenced-in-enclosure for animals, fields for growing crops, and one or more thatched huts. The kraals of my father's wives were separated by many miles and he commuted among them. In these travels, my father sired thirteen children in all, four boys and nine girls. I am the eldest child of the Right Hand House, and the youngest of my father's four sons. I have three sisters, Baliwe, who was the oldest girl, Nontancu and Makhutswana.

When I was not much more than a newborn child, my father was involved in a dispute that deprived him of his chieftainship at Mvezo. … There was no inquiry or investigation; that was reserved for white civil servants. The magistrate simply deposed my father, thus ending the Mandela family chieftainship. … My father, who was a wealthy nobleman by the standards of his time, lost both his fortune and his title. … Because of our straitened circumstances, my mother moved to Qunu, a slightly larger village north of Mvezo, where she would have the support of friends and relations. We lived in less grand style in Qunu, but it was in that village near Umtata that I spent some of the happiest years of my boyhood and whence I traced my earliest memories.

The village of Qunu was situated in a narrow, grassy valley crisscrossed by clear streams, and overlooked by green hills. It consisted of no more than a few hundred people who lived in huts … The huts were generally grouped in a residential area that was some distance away from the maize fields. There were no roads, only paths through the grass worn away by barefoot boys and women. The women and children of the village wore blankets dyed in ochre … Cattle, sheep, goats and horses grazed together in common pastures. … The land itself was owned by the state. With very few exceptions, Africans at that time did not enjoy private title to land in South Africa but were tenants paying rent annually to the government. …

Maize …, sorghum, beans and pumpkin formed the largest portions of our diet not because of any inherent preference for these foods, but because people could not afford anything richer.

The water used for farming, cooking and washing had to be fetched in buckets from streams and springs. This was women's work and, indeed, Qunu was a village of women and children: most of the men spent the greater part of the year working on remote farms or in the mines along the Reef, the great ridge of gold-bearing rock and shale that forms the southern boundary of Johannesburg. They returned perhaps twice a year, mainly to plough the fields. The hoeing, weeding and harvesting were left to the women and the children. Few, if any people in the village knew how to read or write, and the concept of education was still a foreign one to many.

My mother presided over three huts at Qunu, which, as I remember, were always filled with babies and children of my relations. In fact, I hardly recall any occasion as a child when I was alone. In African culture, the sons and daughters of one's aunts or uncles are considered brothers and sisters, not cousins. … We have no half-brothers or half-sisters. My mother's sister is my mother; my uncle's son is my brother; my brother's child is my son, my daughter.

Of my mother's three huts, one was used for cooking, one for sleeping and one for storage. … We slept on mats and sat on the ground. … My mother cooked food in a three-legged iron pot over an open fire in the centre of the hut or outside. Everything we ate we grew and made ourselves. My mother planted and harvested her own mealies. … When preparing the mealies, the women used different methods. They could ground the kernels between two stones to make bread, or boil the mealies first, producing *umphothulo* (mealie flour eaten with sour milk) or *umngqusho* (samp, sometimes plain or mixed with beans). …

From an early age, I spent most of my free time in the veld playing and fighting with the other boys of the village. … From these days I date my love of the veld, of open spaces, the simple beauties of nature, the clean line of the horizon. …

The most popular game for boys was *thinti*, and like most boys' games it was a youthful approximation of war. … After games such as these, I would return to my mother's kraal where she was preparing supper. Whereas my father once told stories of historic battles and heroic Xhosa warriors, my mother would enchant us with Xhosa legends and fables handed over from numberless generations. These tales stimulated my childish imagination, and usually contained some moral lesson. I recall one my mother told us about a traveller who was approached by an old woman with terrible cataracts on her eyes. The women asked the traveller for help, and the man averted his eyes. Then another man came along and was approached by the old woman. She asked him to clean her eyes, and even though he found the task unpleasant, he did as she asked. Then, miraculously, the scales fell from the old woman's eyes and she became young and beautiful. The man married her and became wealthy and prosperous. It is a simple tale, but its message is an enduring one: virtue and generosity will be rewarded in ways that one cannot know.

Like all Xhosa children I acquired knowledge mainly through observation. … My life, and that of most Xhosas at the time, was shaped by custom, ritual and taboo. This was the alpha and omega of our existence, and went unquestioned. Men followed the path laid out for them by their fathers; women led the same lives as their mothers had before them. … I also learned that to neglect one's ancestors would bring ill-fortune and failure in life. … My father did not subscribe to the local prejudice towards the amaMfengu and befriended two amaMfengu brothers, George and Ben Mbekela. The brothers were an exception in Qunu: they were educated and Christian. …

While the faith of the Mbekela brothers did not rub off on my father, it did inspire my mother who became a Christian. In fact, Fanny was literally her Christian name, for she had been given it in church. … One day, George Mbekela paid a visit to my mother. 'Your son is a clever young fellow,' he said. 'He should go to school.' My mother remained silent. No one in my family had ever attended school and my mother was unprepared for Mbekela's suggestion. But she did relay it to my father who, despite – or perhaps because of – his own lack of education, immediately decided that his youngest son should go to school. …

One night, when I was nine years old ... [my father] died. ... Although my mother was the centre of my existence, I defined myself through my father. My father's passing changed my whole life in a way that I did not suspect at the time. After a brief period of mourning, my mother informed me that I would be leaving Qunu. I did not ask her why, or where I was going.

I packed the few things that I possessed and early one morning we set out on a journey westward to my new residence. I mourned less for my father than for the world I was leaving behind. Qunu was all that I knew and I loved it in the unconditional way that a child loves his first home. Before we disappeared behind the hills, I turned and looked for what I imagined was the last time at my village. ... Above all else, my eyes rested on the three simple huts where I had enjoyed my mother's love and protection. It was these three huts that I associated with all my happiness, with life itself, and I rued the fact that I had not kissed each of them before I left. ...

We travelled by foot and in silence until the sun was sinking slowly towards the horizon. But the silence of the heart between mother and child is not a lonely one. My mother and I never talked very much, but we did not need to. I never doubted her love nor questioned her support. ...

Late in the afternoon, at the bottom of a shallow valley surrounded by trees, we came upon a village at the centre of which was a large and gracious home that so far exceeded anything that I had ever seen that all I could do was marvel at it. ... This was the Great Place, Mqhekezweni, ... the royal residence of Chief Jongintaba Dalindyebo, acting regent of the Thembu people.

I learned later that, in the wake of my father's death, Jongintaba had offered to become my guardian. He would treat me as he treated his other children, and I would have the same advantages as they. My mother had no choice; one did not turn down such an overture from the regent. She was satisfied that, although she would miss me, I would have a more advantageous upbringing in the regent's care than in her own.

My mother remained in Mqhekezweni for a day or two before returning to Qunu. Our parting was without fuss. She offered no sermons, no words of wisdom, and no kisses. I suspect she did not want me to feel bereft at her departure and so was matter-of-fact. ... Her tender look was all the affection and support I needed, and as she departed she turned to me and said: *'Uqinis' ufokoto, Kwedini!'* ('Brace yourself, my boy!')

*

Not much is written about Nelson Mandela's mother. Although he did not see his mother regularly, he stayed in contact with her and his sisters. After his first marriage to Evelyn Mase in 1944 his mother came to Johannesburg in 1949 for medical attention and stayed with the couple. In the winter of 1964 Nelson Mandela was sentenced to life in prison. In the space of twelve months between 1968 and 1969, his mother died of a heart attack weeks after visiting him in prison, and his eldest son Madiba Thembekile was killed in a car crash, but he was not allowed to attend the funerals of either.

In a letter dated 1 April 1971 he writes to his sister from the Robben Island prison:

> ... Above all I miss Ma with her kindness and modesty. I thought I loved her when she lived. But it is only now that she is gone that I think I could have spent more time to make her comfortable and happy. You know what I owe to her and the Chief. But how and with what could a prisoner repay a debt owed to the deceased?

Nelson Mandela was born and grew up in the rural areas of the Transkei. His anti-apartheid activities lead to his spending twenty-seven years of his life in jail. He won the Nobel Peace Prize in 1993 and became the first democrati-cally elected president of South Africa in 1994. He passed away 5 December 2013 at Houghton Estate, Johannesburg.

Trevor Manuel

GROWTH AND TRANSFORMATION

Philma Manuel (née Von Söhnen), born 6 June
1926 in Stellenbosch

My father passed away when I was thirteen, leaving my mother as the
only parent responsible for raising me through adolescence and beyond.
She is thirty years older than I am, and we remain very close – the least
I do is speak to her by telephone at least every three days.

Her influence is what I feel very strongly every single day in the
values that I try to live by – even though as an only son, and a rather
mischievous one, I could get away with many things in my youth. There
was a complete intolerance of any breach of the rigid rules that govern
honesty, and to this day, I set so much score by the highest ethical
standards – knowing full well that this is a consequence of my mother's
intolerance of dishonesty.

There were issues that were hard for her to deal with at first – my
decision to give up a 'good job' (the kind that was difficult for township
boys to come by) to become a fulltime activist in 1981; the announce-
ments I made about religion in my youth; my decision to leave home
and move in with a girlfriend – these kinds of decisions were outside
her frame of reference, but once she understood my decisions, and
sometimes had the assurance that a particular decision was not as a
result of failure on her part, she supported me through the decision.

I have seen in her the growth and transformation – from the fear of
the security police to courage in the face of them; from early attempts to
discourage me from participating in political activity to her own activism.
And with this very appreciable transformation came her encouragement of my own activities. This growth compels me to use my mother
as a sounding board, both actually and virtually. For example, there are
very few speeches I make whose rhythm, vocabulary and imagery are
not tested on my mom. Though this does not happen much in real life,

I will talk through the speech, crafting at it as though she is actually present. A useful benchmark for communication of the big issues is the responses of a working-class mother, and that is my mom.

The other values that make for better interaction in political life – such as approaching issues with both feet planted firmly on the ground, never to overpromise, the respect that we must have for all – all of these values I effectively suckled from my mother.

She is an active force in my life and my mental response is to act in a way that will make her proud. I think that we have a deal on that score.

Trevor Manuel was born in Cape Town. He studied civil and structural engineering and later – during his detention, which lasted from 1985 to 1990 – also law. In 1994 he was appointed minister of trade and industry by President Nelson Mandela and in 1996 as minister of finance. He has received numerous international awards and recognition for his accomplishments, such as being selected as a Global Leader for Tomorrow by the World Economic Forum.

Zakes Mda

SIS' ROSE – ROSE MDA

Rose Nompumelelo Mtshula born 23 August 1923 in Queenstown, died 16 September 2006 in Mafeteng, Lesotho

Sis' Rose. That's what the neighbourhood called my mother. Even when she was in her eighties, young women of twenty called her Sis' Rose. By that time she was confined to her bedroom, her joints devastated by arthritis and her memory gradually receding into a very foggy place. This was the time when I flew from America every two months to visit her in a small Lesotho town called Mafeteng where she lived with my brother. She was so beautiful lying on the bed she used to share with my father until he passed on some thirteen years before. She looked so old and frail, Sis' Rose, as women and men of the neighbourhood came and sat in her bedroom for the whole day, conversing among themselves about matters of the village – a discussion in which she could no longer participate.

I never thought my mother could get old. Only other people's mothers got old, not mine. But there she was, Sis' Rose, sitting in the wheelchair I bought her a few years back – the wheelchair she was once reluctant to use because that would be admitting to herself that her legs were gone forever – staring into empty space.

In the evening some of us – her children, daughters-in-law, nieces and nephews, grandchildren – took over the bedroom when the throngs had left, and sang for her, 'Rosie my girl masithandane, sibemoya munye nje ngezingelosi', a syrupy song of past decades in which a man is pleading with a certain Rose that they should fall in love so that their spirits could unite like the spirits of angels.

She loved the attention and she smiled wanly. I admired her beauty as I sang with the rest, and imagined the beautiful young woman who captivated my father decades ago. She and her girlfriends Albertina Sisulu and Evelyn Mase (who later became the first Mrs Mandela) were nursing sisters at a Johannesburg hospital. I have seen the pictures and have always regretted that none of us, her children, inherited her beauty gene – for indeed, we all take after my father's people who are not easy on the eye. Nelson Mandela mentions her in his autobiography, *Long Walk to Freedom*.

As she sat in the wheelchair or lay on the bed with an empty stare, a distant gaze or an impish smile, I could see her in the early sixties in a white nursing sister's starched uniform and maroon 'doubly qualified' epaulettes cycling her way around Dobsonville, visiting the sick at their homes or tending to them at the clinic which was just across the street from our four-roomed township house. At that time she was virtually a single mom, since my father was holed up in the deepest Transkei where he was serving his articles under an attorney called George Matanzima. She had to cope with me, a problem child who often played truant and spent school time playing the pennywhistle at shop verandas or selling sweets in trains. Or fighting in street gangs. One day she beat the hell out of me with a leather belt after a man brought me home screaming and kicking, alleging that I had robbed his daughter whom he had sent to the store. I swore I had not committed the crime, but couldn't convince anyone because I was found with a butcher knife that I had stolen from my mother's very special ivory-handled set. That was the first and the only time my mother ever used corporal punishment on me.

I could see her traversing the mountains and crossing the rivers of southern Lesotho in a small van, tending patients and delivering babies, after her family had been exiled to Lesotho in 1963. She was a nursing sister at a Roman Catholic Church clinic at Holy Cross. When her varicose veins caught up with her, she had to give that up. She opened two cafés in Mafeteng and thrived as a small business woman. But she continued to be our nurse, giving us injections at the slightest hint of flu.

I could see her reading the manuscripts of my novels. I was working at Yale University in the United States when I wrote my first novel, *Ways of Dying*. After writing every chapter I would mail it to her in Lesotho. She would read it and mail me back her comments. It was like I was writing it for her. I aimed to make her laugh and I succeeded. Even though I was writing about death it became an upbeat novel. The same process happened with my second novel, *She Plays with the Darkness*. I was in Vermont when I wrote the first few chapters, but completed it when I had returned to Johannesburg. I enjoyed the moments when I drove to Lesotho, taking her new chapters and looking forward to discussing the chapters she had already read. She simply loved Tampololo, a very fish-wifey character I had created, basing her on someone I had brought into the family and who had turned out to be the bane of our lives. By the time I wrote my third novel, *The Heart of Redness*, her eyes were failing her, yet she still wanted the manuscripts and asked her constant visitors from the neighbourhood to read them to her. She was a daughter of the Cwerha Gxarha clan, descendants of the Khoikhoi people, and was pleased that they featured in my story. For the rest of my novels I missed her comments, and always felt that something was missing in them: she.

I remember her joy when she finally met her dearest friends, Walter and Albertina Sisulu, after decades of separation. One day their daughter-in-law, Elinor, brought them to my house at Weltevredenpark, Roodepoort, to meet her, and this was surely one of the highlights of her old and ailing life.

Then one Saturday, sitting on her trusty chair, she nodded off and left us. Silently. The girl from next door was with her.

Zakes Mda is a novelist, poet and playwright who is also a painter, composer and filmmaker. He was born in Herschel in the Eastern Cape and studied and worked in South Africa, Lesotho and the United Kingdom. He went into exile and returned to South Africa in 1995. He now commutes between South Africa and the USA, working as professor of creative writing in the English Department at Ohio University, beekeeper in the Eastern Cape and adviser to the Market Theatre, Johannesburg.

Dirk Meerkotter

DEVIATING FROM THE RECIPE

Anna Sophia Meerkotter (née Pelser), born
12 June 1927 in Johannesburg

Anna Sophia Meerkotter (née Pelser) was born on 12 June 1927 and grew up in Norwood, Johannesburg. She had a very good relationship with Nico Pelser, her father, who taught her to interrogate what was happening in our society, to question, and to think. Her father took part in the 1914 Rebellion against South Africa's participation in the Great War on the side of the British, which led to his imprisonment. Nico Pelser passed away in 1942 as a result of a chronic kidney-related illness that he contracted in a British concentration camp as a child. His illness and subsequent death forced Annie to take up a secretarial position at the age of fourteen to support her mother and older sister and to provide food and shelter for her three younger sisters and her brother.

Annie Meerkotter's own upbringing and education was reflected in our home, where the dinner table became a place for discussions, debates and questions. Annie's intellectual openness not only contributed to the development of her own five children, but also supported my artistic father, who developed into a prolific abstract and contemporary South African painter. My father often referred to my mother as his strictest, yet, at the same time, most constructive critic.

Annie set an excellent example for her children to study. In her mid-twenties, she matriculated with a first-class pass and two distinctions. Her studies did not end with her matriculation certificate. She was awarded a BA degree with History of Art as a major in 1968, the year after I completed my BA degree.

The story would, however, be incomplete without mentioning the extraordinary compassion she displayed towards all the individuals she had contact with. In spite of encouraging us to challenge and interrogate those ideas that we were confronted with, she taught us not to be judgemental and to respect the rights of others whose ideas might differ from our own views about life and living. Except when those ideas were in conflict with the principle of respect for the basic rights of other human beings. Much of this ethos of treating fellow human beings in the same way that one would expect to be treated by others is a combination of those things which she learned from her father, as well as from the warmth and love my grandmother, and Annie's mother, shared with those around her.

As a homemaker par excellence, Annie Meerkotter had the gift of making all those around her feel welcome and cared for. I can't remember times when we did not have a financially, and/or personally distressed person or family member in our home. Supported by her husband, Dirk, she was always ready to care for those who experienced woes which were difficult to come to terms with.

My mother also taught us that the heart and the mind are not to be separated into two different categories. Her reflections about existential questions we in South Africa were confronted with on a daily basis were always aimed at addressing those things which made it difficult for fellow human beings to see the light at the end of the tunnel and to assist them in confronting the challenges they were faced with in a dignified manner.

In the case of both my mother and my father, it became clear to me at an early stage in my life that the roles of fathers and mothers ought not to be stereotyped along so-called male-dominated ways of doing and thinking in the case of fathers, and female-oriented forms of behaviour in the case of mothers. In our home, both parents' lives made it clear to their children that the affective, as well as the intellectual and rational, form part of the relationships all human beings establish with their neighbours.

In the heyday of apartheid education, when my younger brothers and I attended school, my mother's views were not commonly accepted. Generally speaking, women were not to ask challenging questions, whereas music and art were viewed very differently from rugby, boxing and wrestling when it came to the role fathers had to play in the upbringing of their children. Especially so in the case of their sons. My parents' obvious acknowledgment of the importance of the heart and the mind in the upbringing of their children complemented the examples they set for us very well, to say the least.

Although it might be obvious that my father's paintings, which certainly differed from the typical South African landscapes with a farm-house in the shadow of Australian bluegum trees and distant moun-tains in the background, influenced us to see things in different ways, my mother's creative cooking was also unusually stimulating and challenging.

From an educational perspective, the daily ways of doing things in the home have a remarkable influence on children's development. In a home where something like traditional cooking may tend to entrench much more than the ways in which one thinks about food, my mother's deviations from the recipe, in hindsight, have undoubtedly, fundamentally influenced her children's views on the meaning of life. Her sons were encouraged to bake cakes and make food since their primary school days, with the focus on interesting new tastes rather than following the rules laid down by the recipe books that tended to result in predictable outcomes. Many of our friends found these cooking exercises very exciting, even though they were not necessarily allowed to engage in such non-masculine activities in their own homes.

Food and the discussions at the dinner table were, as I have men-tioned before, important in our home. The discussions often created the opportunity to put some of the one-sided views that we were exposed to in our classrooms in a different perspective. One of the many lessons about the dangers of being judgemental that I can recall originated from a discussion that we had had at school about Christianity and Islam. Implied in this discussion was that the Almighty of the Bible was the only god and different from, for example, the Allah of the Muslims. Instead of giving a straight answer to the comments and questions we had about the discussion, my mother, again, warned us about the dan-gers of being judgemental and ended the discussion with the following question: Might it not be that the Jews, Christians and Muslims refer to the same god, taking into consideration that their religions originated in the same part of the world? On the whole, the majority of discussions at the dinner table ended with questions rather than answers.

To this day, her understanding of what human beings are about remains one which meaningfully addresses the existential questions that we, as human beings generally and South Africans more specifically, are faced with on a daily basis. One has a moral obligation to work towards the creation of the same space for those of us who have not had the opportunity to think about who we are and where we might be going in an environment built on respect for diverse views and an unconditional love for those around us.

Professor Dirk Meerkotter is the firstborn child of Annie and Dirk Meerkotter, the artist. In 2005 he retired as dean of the Faculty of Education at the University of the Western Cape and has published widely over the past three decades in the fields of curriculum, teacher education, emancipatory action research, language education, HIV/AIDS in education and critical pedagogy. He is currently documenting his father's life and well-acknowledged work as a South African artist.

Piet Meiring

A CROSS AGAINST THE WINDOW

Sophia Gerhardina Meiring (née Kloppers),
born 17 June 1905 in Machadodorp, died
13 August 2003 in Pretoria

We were waiting at Heidelberg station for my father to come home – my mother, my four sisters, myself, a couple of school mates as well as our two dogs – Baron the Labrador and Klasie the fox terrier. In the train compartment, as my father told us on our way home, a very friendly lady had been making his acquaintance. She had seemed more than willing to get to know him better – not realising that he was a Dutch Reformed pastor returning to his flock after attending a synodical meeting in Pretoria. But when the train stopped and the band of children, animals and a smiling wife started running towards the train to embrace my father, who had been away for a full twenty-four hours, he overheard his travel companion sighing with relief: 'Good Lord – what an escape!'

This is the fondest memory I have of my mother: laughing, gathering her children and their friends around her and embracing her husband. She could have been many other things in her life. She may have followed an academic career. During her student days at Wits University she received many accolades and awards. During her life she served on many councils and committees, wrote a number of books and was in great demand as a public speaker. For more than twenty years she had a weekly slot in *Vrouerubriek*, the SABC's Afrikaans programme for women. But her heart belonged to us, her family.

I remember her as the teller of stories. At night she would sit with us children, regaling us with yet another episode from the adventures of Elsa and Hilda, my sisters' imaginary heroines, or Dingesie ('Whats-his-name'), my best pal who ran into mischief and trouble daily, often to be rescued in the nick of time. The stories were always fun, preparing us for bed. Come to think of it, Mother sometimes dozed off with us, in the middle of her story. From time to time her tales were about her own travels. As a young teacher she had quit her job for seven months to travel the world with three lady companions, sailing by boat to Australia and New Zealand and on to the United States and Europe. Some of her experiences were hair-raising. Imagine her on a train in Germany, in 1936, in a heated argument with a number of Nazi officers, on how Hitler had it all wrong and needed to be stopped.

After marrying my father in 1937 her role changed dramatically from adventurer to *pastoriemoeder* (pastor's wife), initially in Rondebosch, and then in Johannesburg, Heidelberg and Pretoria. In Heidelberg, with its large farming community, she turned into a veritable chef, cooking bobotie and seaweed jelly, canning baskets full of apricots, quince and peaches, proudly presenting her home-grown tomatoes at the annual agricultural show. And, above all, making sure that not a precious drop of milk from Vaseline, our very productive cow, was left unused. Milk in the morning, milk at lunch and milk porridge in the evenings!

The doors of the manse were open to all – to family and friends, to parishioners and to students from the teachers' training college who either needed guidance in their personal lives or help with yet another assignment put to them by the lecturers. My mother enjoyed people. 'Loving God means loving his children' was her motto; reach out to others, try to understand and to meet their needs were some of the lessons she instilled in us. In a room full of guests she would look for an outsider and join him or her in conversation or, with a raised eyebrow, direct one of us to do the same. She had lots of practical advice to give. One of her favourites was quoting a friend who used to say, 'Look, if my daughter-in-law fries her fish in lamp oil, I will still call it delicious!' On one memorable occasion she had the current prime minister of South Africa, with two of his successors (Dr DF Malan, Advocate JG Strijdom and Dr HF Verwoerd) for tea in our lounge and with great flair directed the flow of local dignitaries who dropped by to greet the famous men.

Mother had her faults. She could get flustered and irritable if things went wrong. There were times when she was quite angry with her children, and said so, only to embrace us minutes later, pleading with us to forgive her. I remember my boyhood shock – and secret admiration – when on rare occasions she would be heard mumbling 'Dash it!' In our home, where we never heard our dominee father use strong language, the expletive sounded deliciously sinful.

At the end of his life my father suffered from Parkinson's disease, but Mother helped him carry his burden with patience and with humour. And when, after his death, she moved to a retirement home, she continued as always: delivering koeksisters and pastries to the ill and infirm, brewing coffee every evening for the night watchmen, and – above all – telling stories to her growing number of grandchildren and great-grandchildren.

Mother's imprint on my own life is vast. When I, as a young dominee in the Dutch Reformed Church, started to question the morality of apartheid and the church's theological defence of the policy of separate development, she was very supportive. When I, from time to time, ran into trouble because of it, she was indignant! It was, after all, she and my father who taught us to love and respect God's children from all communities. And when, years later, I was invited to join the Truth and Reconciliation Commission, she wrote me a very beautiful letter with a heartfelt prayer for the Commission and for me that I will treasure for the length of my days.

George Bernard Shaw once said that the world's population might be divided into two groups: the teachers and the doers. Mother, it seems to me, had a measure of both. Her faith in God was firm and very practical. In one of her books she recalled her visit to New Zealand's South Island. High up in the mountains she and her friends happened on a small church, with a large window behind the altar. The picture was imprinted on her mind: the altar with the wooden cross against the backdrop of the incredibly beautiful snow-covered mountains. Without the image of the cross of Christ, the beautiful scene would have been erased from my mind many years ago. But with the cross in the foreground it became a symbol of the gospel message. If we see our lives against the cross, what a beautiful panorama it becomes! All the valleys of suffering, the lakes of peace, the precipices of struggle and the mountain tops of victory begin to make sense – become a miracle of God.

Sophie Meiring passed away in Pretoria at the age of ninety-eight. At her funeral, the church was filled with people, young and old, whose lives had been touched by hers, who had experienced her joyous embrace. She had asked me, days before, to conduct the service. My message was given to me: Mother's life, with the cross of Jesus Christ in the forefront, presented a beautiful panorama to all who knew her.

Professor Piet Meiring was born in Johannesburg. He studied at the University of Pretoria, as well as at the Free University, Amsterdam. Ordained to the ministry of the Dutch Reformed Church in 1968, he has been heavily involved in the church's struggle against apartheid – challenging his own denomination in this regard. He was invited to join the South African Truth and Reconciliation Commission (1996–1998) as a committee member of the Reparations and Rehabilitation Committee. In 1999 he was appointed director of the Centre for Theology and Community in the Theological Faculty of the University of Pretoria.

Elana Meyer

THE ATTITUDE OF BELIEF

Ene van Zyl (née Lombaard), born 3 January
1936 in Cradock

I grew up in Albertinia, a small town in the Western Cape. I was one of four children. We lived on a farm five kilometres outside Albertinia. At an early age I ran pretty well and participated in the local fun runs, then went on a coaching course where I discovered that I had a little bit of talent.

And now, when I look back, being a mother myself with my little son Christopher, I can see how brave it was of my mother to give me the opportunity at a pretty young age to go to boarding school to be able to train for my running. I went to Robertson where I was coached by Charly Faasen, my school coach.

These were the two major, major influences in my life, the people who gave me the opportunity to pursue a career in running: my mother and my coach. And I think it is my mother's attitude that made me succeed. For her, nothing is impossible. I think she just believes any-thing is possible. I got that belief from her: I never believe something is impossible.

She taught me that it is better to try something and fail than not try anything. And I think that is probably my best quality, definitely as a sportsperson. Because of her I was never scared of failing. I think a lot of kids are too scared to try; they would rather not try and be unsuccessful than give it a try. This way they never give themselves an opportunity to fail, and keep on living in a very safe zone.

My mother always set big parameters or big boundaries for me to explore. So it was always a safe space, but I never felt claustrophobic. I could always explore, more and more within those safe boundaries. I think what she has given me mainly is an attitude, an attitude of belief: belief in faith.

My mother comes from the Eastern Cape. She was born in 1937 in Cradock, where she grew up. She went to Wellington College boarding school, which was a girls' school, and then to Normaal College Pretoria (NKP) to study.

They were three siblings at home. She was the oldest, having a sister and a younger brother. She finished her matric at the age of fifteen or sixteen years and then went to Normaal College to study Physical Education. In those days travelling was not that easy. She had to take the train to Pretoria, but she was very determined. She started teaching at the very young age of eighteen years at a very small farm school in Albertinia. She was the Standard Three teacher but she also coached netball and other sports for high school kids. Some of those high school kids were almost as old as she. She took the school's netball team to being the best in South Western District, and really made an impact as a sports teacher. These are not things I knew about her then; it's only later, when you start talking to your mother and relatives, that you come to know these details. Recently one of my cousins told me that my mom was a very good hurdler when she was at NKP. Apparently one weekend when there were trials, she went back home to the Western Cape, because she lived far from school, and missed the trials. That weekend a runner slower than her was accepted into the team.

Obviously she has sporting genes, but when I look at her, I see she has more than that: family is important to her, life is important, more so than just sporting opportunities.

She chose family above sport, but she did have the genes.

She gave me the opportunity and supported me at the very young age of twelve years when I had to go to boarding school. Most parents don't have the courage to do that. In terms of sport, if it had not been for her and her courage, my life would have been very different. By going to boarding school I entered a new sphere of opportunity by having a very good school coach and becoming part of the Western Province team. Charly Faasen invested in me as a person and not only as an athlete. Because of my mother's courage, I had the opportunity to be coached and mentored by someone very special. Back then I did not see it as something special, it was almost like a natural next step for me, but if I look back now, I am aware that I was given an amazing opportunity which shaped my world in many ways.

I did not really know my grandparents on my mother's side very well. They lived in Cradock and we sometimes went there to visit them during holiday when I was little. My grandmother passed away the year before I went to school and my grandfather one year later. I remember that day. It was in 1973, just before we moved into our new house. One evening I fell over some building equipment and broke my nose and I remember that that had been the very same night we got the news that my grandfather had passed away.

I don't know if they were very sporty, but my grandparents had a farm where my mother grew up. They also had a tennis court on the farm. When we were adults my mom still played tennis for Albertinia, and all her sisters' kids are good sports people.

She met my dad, a young farmer, when she started teaching, but they did not get married until some years later. I was born when my mother was thirty years old. My sister is two years older than I and my parents got married just before she was born. So she must have been a teacher for quite a time before she got married.

I am the second child. I have one older sister, a brother two years younger and another younger sister. There is a two-year age difference between each of us.

My older sister was very strong academically and she too did a lot of sport growing up. My brother and my younger sister both ran. My brother also played rugby very well. He played on senior level for Boland and my younger sister ran as well, even faster than me at a younger age. Then she went to university and did not pursue it further. So there are obviously genes in the family that show we can do sport.

When we were growing up it seemed to us that my mother had the energy to do everything. She was a teacher till the age of sixty-five. When she does something, it almost turns to gold – at least this was my perception. By observing her and her faith you start believing that things will always work out. You are never scared of trying lest you might fail. I think she set a daily example while we were growing up. She took a break when we were born until my youngest sister went to school. Then she started teaching again and worked as a headmaster of a school in a coloured farming community. She drove sixty kilometres every day on a farm road, changing her own tires when she had a flat. After she got home she still had a zillion other things to do. I never had the feeling that life was too busy or even challenging for her.

And now that I am in a similar position, having Christopher and having a job, it almost feels as if I do not have time for myself. Now I really appreciate what my mother did for us. We were four kids and I start wondering, How did she do it with four kids, plus a fulltime job? How did she stay sane? She did it with flying colours; I can't think of her ever complaining once.

She also baked bread. At home this is not part of my portfolio. My partner Jacques has to put in as many cooking hours as I do. Except for braais, my dad never cooked dinner; he was a farmer and was always busy on the farm. Now I ask myself sometimes when I don't have time for myself, How did my mom manage to do all that?

My mother was very tough, even towards men. Older, grey-haired men told me this about her. She used to give us a good hiding, she was a tough mom, but that is not what I remember about her – other people remind me that she also had this side.

My mother was never the 'driver of the dreams', she just wanted to be supportive. You get so many parents who have unfulfilled dreams and whose children do sport not because they want to but because they want to please their parents. My mom was never like that, but she always supported me to go to events and to races – and always somehow made it possible for me. If I had to go to national championships, it was never an issue at home that we might not be able to afford it, although I did not grow up in a wealthy family. It always just happened and somehow I always got the opportunity to go.

And my parents were always there to watch; they both went to all the events.

They also went to the Barcelona Olympic Games. It was the only international event they attended; it was the only time in their lives that they travelled abroad. It was so nice that they had the opportunity to accompany me. For Barcelona, we did not have a lot of time to prepare. I knew only in April 1992 that sport unified. So we did not know whether we were going and could only book very late. My parents had to stay one hour outside Barcelona and had to take a train to travel into the city every morning. Once, when they tried to catch their train back, my mother fell and broke her arm on one of the platforms. It was late, so in the middle of the night she had to go to a doctor. She did not let me know about it because she did not want to upset me. And I was so cross with her for not telling me – not knowing made me upset. It was very special to have my parents in Barcelona. Very, very special!

Now my mom and my dad are both retired. They lived on their farm till last year and then moved to Godous River Mouth. They love it there. I am glad to see how content and happy they are, just waking up to the sound of the sea. But my mom is still not able to take it easy. She is already part of the community. Every week they have a book club and a kettle club – she is already involved in so many community activities.

Many people grow old and feel purposeless or depend heavily on their children to make them happy. Not my parents – they love spending time with us, especially now that Christopher is here. I have never felt that it is my responsibility to make sure that they are happy. My parents are very self-sufficient. My mom has always been that way.

Because of her, I believe that I can be whatever I want to be. The biggest thing a mother can pass on to you is that you can set goals in life and follow a direction. If I want to achieve something, I have to follow the steps to get there. It's a simple philosophy. I learnt this through sport also and I honour it in my everyday life – and I am consistent. This is an attitude I learnt from my mom.

Elana Meyer grew up in the rural areas of the Western Cape. She has been among the world's elite athletes for over ten years, won a silver medal for South Africa in the 10 000 metres at the Barcelona Olympics in 1992 and remains one of the world's best half-marathon and marathon runners.

Wally Morrow

A GOOD START

Eugenie Leonie Blake, born 28 January 1912 in Pretoria, died 30 January 1998 in Pretoria

When I hear evangelical people propounding moral lessons, or politicians promoting 'family values', it offends me. This might seem paradoxical in the light of the fact that I think that moral action is the basis of a good and satisfying human life, and that there can be little more important in growing up than finding oneself in a nurturing and loving family.

Two possible explanations for this paradox spring to mind. One is that my mother was quietly sceptical about sermons and homilies; the other is my vivid consciousness of the ways in which colonialism and apartheid disrupted the family life of many fellow South Africans, and the way that at this time HIV and AIDS and poverty are depriving many South Africans, particularly those who are young, of the privileges of growing up in families and with mothers.

If they were significant presences in our lives during our dawning awareness of ourselves and the world, it is far from easy to write about our mothers (or grandmothers) and the kind of influence they had on our lives. Their influence is woven into the tapestry of who we are. Such influence is exceptionally difficult to disentangle from our sense of our own personal identity, or to articulate in terms of causes and effects (a mode that is the bread and butter of good historians). I will try, in the disengaged style of a historian, to begin with a brief historical account of my mother's origins and life.

My mother was born Eugenie Leonie Blake in January 1912, and she died two days after her eighty-sixth birthday, in 1998. She was born and died in Pretoria, and apart from a brief few years in Durban (and Isipingo), lived her life in Pretoria. Depending on how one counts, she was at least a fifth-generation South African. Her ancestry was nineteenth-century German and English, with repeated local inputs generation after generation.

My mother's paternal great-great-grandfather, John Blake, arrived in the Cape in 1806 with the British army. He married a local Cape Town girl, Susanna Buissine. Their son married Elizabeth Bedford (mixed local Dutch and English), and they moved to Knysna in the 1830s. Their son, Arthur George Blake (my mother's grandfather), born in the 1840s, and his wife, Clara Francina Knobel, had a son, John Blake, in Grahamstown in 1874. He was destined to become my mother's father. The family moved to Pretoria (by oxwagon) in 1888, where they established a successful auctioneering and property development business and became quite affluent. In 1899, at the outbreak of war, John Blake (at the age of twenty-five) found himself in a difficult situation. As a citizen of the ZAR he was called up for military service against the British. He headed for Colesberg where he sat out the war until the British took Pretoria. The British had commandeered the Blake properties, and their business suffered further during the severe recession that followed the war.

My mother's maternal grandfather, Johann Norgarb, born and bred in Germany, arrived in Clanwillaim as a missionary in 1850. He married Elsie van Zijl, a local girl from Calvinia, and they had about a dozen children. Their eldest daughter, Elsie Johanna (Norgarb), born in 1872, was my mother's mother. After the death of Johann Norgarb in 1900, the family moved to Pretoria (where one of the children had a job) and my mother's mother became, in effect, the housekeeper and childminder of the younger children of the marriage.

In 1905 Elsie Norgarb and John Blake were married in Pretoria. They produced three sons and two daughters, one of whom died in infancy, the other was my mother, born when her mother was forty.

My mother and father had known each other for some years prior to their marriage. They were married in 1936, and produced five children, a daughter, a son (me) and three further daughters. My father was born in Pietermaritzburg in 1909, one of the sons of Irish immigrants. The Morrow family ran into financial difficulties and moved to Pretoria in about 1912. My father started work at the age of fourteen to assist with the parlous family income. When he was twenty, in 1929, the Great Depression overtook families, and they had to hold on to whatever paid employment they had, however low the wages.

My mother must have been an exceptionally diligent pupil. She attended a Jewish primary school in Pretoria and Pretoria Girls' High School, where she matriculated in 1928 at the age of seventeen. It was unusual for a girl to matriculate at that time. During her younger years she learnt how to play the piano and until a late age she remained a talented pianist with a great love of both playing and listening to music. After school she trained as a shorthand typist and worked for various businesses in Pretoria until the time of her marriage in 1936. She had excellent handwriting and was a reliably accurate speller and a fluent writer. In these respects she set the bar at a level of which I have always fallen short. She was an inspiring writer of letters who kept up a constant stream of communication with her offspring as they moved out of home and her more distant relatives and friends. Her letters were like small works of art and a delight to read, filled with news about members of the family and their doings, and a constant reinforcement of family bonds.

After her marriage she never again took a paid job. She unselfishly devoted her whole married life to maintaining a calm and nurturing family home. She was always there when we needed her, with constant support and encouragement for all her children. Four years after her marriage, and having produced two children (one of whom was me), the Second World War intervened. My father became a soldier and for a year was sent to Nairobi. My mother was left in Pretoria with two young children. Eventually she persuaded my father to get a transfer to Durban. At first we lived in rather seedy 'residential hotels' and then in a rented house in Isipingo. In retrospect it is clear to me that my mother wanted to maintain the family bonds, especially during the growing and impressionable years of the two youngest children, even in the face of financial stringencies.

She herself enjoyed reading and frequently read to her children but was often so busy with housework and other chores that she didn't have as much time to read as she said she would have liked. She had an infectious sense of humour and delighted in verbal jokes, riddles, irony, funny songs and all the tricks that language play, something which I can see in my own stance toward the world. Her humour extended to other forms of pranks and practical jokes. Perhaps she picked up this characteristic from her Norgarb uncles, who were young men at the time she was growing up and very much part of her original family circle. She would talk about the 'madman' (Eugène Marais) who lived a few doors away from them in Beatrix Street and from whom she and her brothers used to hide behind the hedge, watching him and trying to suppress their mirth as he walked up and down the pavement in his peculiar manner, muttering to himself.

But despite her love of fun she suffered three traumatic experiences which added a darker dimension to her view of human life. Soon after completing her own matric her younger brother, of whom she was deeply fond, was repeating his matric year for the second time when quite suddenly and unexpectedly he developed meningitis. He died within two days. Shortly after she had been married she was looking after a seven-year-old girl cousin of mine (one of her brothers' children) for the afternoon. During the night this little girl suddenly developed gastro-enteritis and died before the morning. My mother felt guilty about this tragedy for the remainder of her life, convinced that she had somehow been responsible. And she cared for her own mother during a long and distressing illness before she died. My mother was thirty-three at the time. She thought that fate could deal you a bad hand but that you had to do the best you could, whatever cards you were dealt.

She shared her sense of fun with her children and grandchildren and would descend into irrepressible fits of giggles when she noticed something amusing or ironical. And her sense of fun was infectious; all her children and grandchildren recall occasions on which my mother would notice something amusing and drag children into the zone of uncontrollable hilarity. These shared giggling bouts were vivid moments of extraordinarily deep and mutual communication. She somehow managed to convey to children how unique and special each of them was, and made them feel good about themselves. Until the very last days of her life she was astonishingly good at communicating with young children and establishing an extraordinary kind of intimate contact with them. She seemed to tune into their wavelength intuitively and understood what they were interested in, and what they would find amusing.

The combination of a sense of fun and fate was one of the central features of my mother's character, and this is something I see in my own life. My mother had strong aspirations for her children to make the best of what life had offered them. I never had any doubt what I should do after (miraculously) completing matric. Despite the fact that funds were not readily available my mother would have liked her children to continue studying after matric. In my case it was a matter of accepting a state loan to train as a teacher. My mother never pushed us, but was proud of our achievements. She hated people she called 'snobs'; people who 'took themselves too seriously' or thought of themselves as superior to those around them. She herself was modest and self-effacing and did not go in for boasting or self-promotion. When I consider this I see characteristics of this kind weaving through my life.

My mother was an exemplary listener. I suppose this is one aspect of her love of reading. She heard what others were saying, at a very profound level, and was an ideal model of a genuine communicator. She had her own strong opinions about most matters, including the political matters of the day, but she expertly used soft power as opposed to violence and the strident tone of the self-righteous. These are characteristics I can see in my own career.

My mother was never deliberately unkind to anyone or anything, had a strong belief in the importance of honesty and sincerity and was the most unselfish person I have ever known. She hated pretentiousness and self-importance, was modest about her not inconsiderable talents and achievements, and was not one to blow her own trumpet. But I think, most importantly, what I inherited from her was a strong conviction that values are to be lived rather than spoken about.

Wally Morrow is one of South Africa's most respected thinkers in education. Born in Pretoria, he was formerly professor of Philosophy of Education and dean of Education at the University of the Western Cape, dean of Education at the University of Port Elizabeth and chair of the Ministerial Committee on Teacher Education. Since the early 1990s he has been prominently involved in transforming South African education and he has played a leading role in guiding the education sector's response to HIV/AIDS in Sub-Saharan Africa. To his regret, he was no longer able to continue with this important work since becoming ill in February 2008. He passed away in 2009.

Cedric Nunn

MADHLAWU

Amy 'Madhlawu' Louw (1900–2003),
born in the Ceza region, Natal

It was a photographic project in the early eighties that led me back to reconnect with my maternal grandmother, Amy 'Madhlawu' Louw. She lived in the remote region of iVuna, midway between Ulundi and Nongoma, KwaZulu-Natal. She was born in 1900 and raised in the nearby Ceza region. Her father, Arthur Nicholson, had come from England as a soldier in the British army fighting in the Anglo-Zulu War, and at the end of the conflict somehow remained in Zululand, marrying Elina Velaphi Mabaso, a Zulu woman.

I had the good fortune of seeing quite a lot of my grandmother while I was growing up, as we were living about a hundred kilometres away in Hluhluwe. I spent several holidays with her and we frequently visited her over weekends. But for a child growing up, adults were remote and not easily accessible. When I returned years later as a thirty-year-old, I began to see her and the land she inhabited with fresh eyes and new understanding. Encountering her as an adult, in what I had regarded as a harsh and unforgiving landscape, far from the conveniences of civilisation, I immediately began to see how truly remarkable she was.

Madhlawu had had two marriages, first to Willy Louw when she was about twenty, then, after Willy had died, to his brother Dandy when she was in her forties. When we teased her about this seemingly traditional practice she was quick to tell us that she married him for love and that he was the sweetest man. From these two unions she produced eight children, five from her first marriage and three from the second. She kept all her pregnancies through to term and raised all her children in that remote region.

She was already in her eighties when I re-encountered her in my thirties, and had had to relocate to higher ground after the death of her second husband Dandy, when the land they had occupied was designated communal grazing ground by the local chief. She left the solid stone house built by her husbands and built what was to be a temporary house, of wattle and daub, about two kilometres away from the confluence of the iVuna and White Umfolozi where the stone house was.

It was in this humble abode, where she was to live for the rest of her life, that I began once again to make her acquaintance. I spent a week with her on that first encounter, rising with her in the morning and heading into the fields, returning at midday to eat lunch and then taking a siesta in the fierce heat of the day. A peasant farmer, she was incredibly resourceful and enterprising.

Her days were filled with planting maize, sorghum, pumpkins and cotton, hoeing, feeding fowls, ducks and pigs, making grass mats, sewing clothes to sell, brewing Zulu beer (for which she was renowned), selling snuff from the tobacco she grew and of course the inevitable cleaning and cooking in her own home. In addition to all this there was the constant flow of neighbours and visitors who kept her informed of events in the community. There was always time to relax in the midday heat and to enjoy company in the cool of the afternoons and evenings. Radio Zulu was a constant background sound.

I found that she occupied a space that did not quite fit in with the orthodoxy of the apartheid eighties. The only person of mixed race in her immediate environment, she was surrounded by Zulu neighbours and in many ways shared a life with them. But there was this curious reserve, a contradiction that confounded me, a certain distancing. For instance, MaKhumalo, her closest neighbour and friend, would never sit on a chair whilst visiting. Instead, she would sit on the floor or stand, showing a definite deference.

My mother explained that when Granny had arrived in this region, which was largely unpopulated, in the thirties, the people who lived around her had come there originally mostly as servants. Whilst Granny's husbands were alive, they had had many cattle and were considered wealthy by the standards of the time. Therefore there was a class difference which continued to be observed by all, even after the loss of all her cattle through a cattle disease that ravaged the land and the relocation that had reduced what little of the herd had remained.

As a child, I had obviously seen her quite differently: as a distant elder who occasionally was able to give me, one of very many grand-children, some attention. As an adult, I was able to see in her the things I was unable to see as a child. She was a reserved person, but readily engaged when necessary. She quietly accepted the circumstances life threw at her and rarely let them get her down. My respect for her grew as I began to comprehend the complexity of her environment and the simplicity she had brought to bear in relating to it.

From what I observed, there seemed to be a sliver of a way of life that could have been lived in harmony and mutual interdependence between people – people who readily observed class difference but recognised their blood ties – had it not been for the meddling of the apartheid social experiment of group separation. I discovered that Madhlawu had Zulu relatives in the nearby region, though I never got to meet them until much later. Her Zulu mother was from the region, and Madhlawu retained a connection with her maternal family.

In all this time she lived a solitary life, well into her nineties, being visited from time to time by her children who had all moved to the cities, and occasionally visiting them. Her independent spirit (she resisted every effort of ours to have her relocate to seemingly more convenient locales) inspired me as well. My mother and our family were sympa-thetic and supportive of her wish to remain in her own home even as she became infirm with old age, and my mother made great sacrifices to spend long stretches of time with her, doing what she considered her daughterly duties.

What she valued in her life, which was lived close to the earth, reso-nates with our emerging understanding of the wisdom of growing one's own food and consuming food from within a five-kilometre radius from where one lives. Intuitively, she lived this life. Her refusal to eat commer-cially raised chicken is well known in our family. She was also notorious for her sharp tongue that would spare no fool, and she lived up to her local name of Madhlawu, which means 'the sharp-tongued one'.

Madhlawu loved a good drinking session and, even more so, a party. But she could live with the remains of whatever alcohol was not used up in that session in her house for months until another occasion presented itself. Even when well into her eighties, she would delight all present by dancing a jig and singing a song about being sixteen, young and pretty.

I believe I was fortunate to be raised in a community that valued the aged, a view that is so different from the prevalent one in the Western civilised world in which old people's lives are seen as being wasted and over, fit only to be spent in an old-age home. In Madhlawu's world, old age commanded respect and inclusion and she, though constantly referring to herself as being old, commanded the status of equal.

She gave respect as readily as she expected it. And whilst I can see how the rigid imposition of the perspective of old people, especially where it is out of step with the youth, could be constricting, there is a need for balance in which the value of all ages is maintained. This I learned from Madhlawu.

Our matriarch is now gone. She died with dignity at the age of a hundred-and-three, in the arms of her last few remaining children. The family, who are struggling to find a new centre in the wake of the gap that her parting has left, keenly feels her departure. The home she created and maintained is gone and with it our connection to the 'old country'. But something remains that she has established, a pattern, perhaps, of possibilities, of ways of being, that transcends narrow boundaries. For that I thank her.

Cedric Nunn, born in Nongoma, KwaZulu-Natal, is a photographer. He began taking photos in the early eighties, initially documenting the realities of apartheid that seemed to have been ignored by the mainstream media. His focus throughout his work has been on recording social change.

Aziz Pahad

AN ORDINARY WOMAN WITH A VISION

Amina Pahad, born 1918 in Klerksdorp, died
1973 in Mumbai

My mother Amina Pahad, born in July 1918 in Klerksdorp in the then
Transvaal, was an ordinary woman of Indian descent who was inspired
by extraordinary ideals. Though she never sought the limelight, through
her struggle and her political defiance she exemplified the dogged
belief in the possibility of building a different society, one imbued with
notions of love for humanity, irrespective of colour, caste, creed or race.
Her vision, like ours today, was of a non-racial, non-sexist, democratic
South Africa.

My mother was first a humanist who displayed immense strength
and courage in the face of adversity. She was a feminist before contemporary ideas of feminism had taken root. Her feminism drew from the
wellspring of her deep and abiding commitment to human rights and
social justice – ideals which she assiduously cultivated in all of us. She
was kind and generous even when our entire family was continually
harassed by the then notorious Special Branch who, with regularity
and at all hours of the day and night, came to our flat in Becker Street,
Johannesburg. When they arrived at our flat she was polite and patient
with them. She fed them, gave them coffee and tea and when we complained that they were there to arrest any one of us, she simply asked
us, as a rebuke, 'Whose house is this, yours or mine?' To my mother they
were 'only doing their job'. She treated them as she would any other
visitor entering our home.

To all in the neighbourhood her hallmarks, her strengths, were her
kindness, her generosity of spirit, her selflessness and her commitment

to community. She saw no contradiction between her commitment to family and community and her commitment to fighting oppression and discrimination. If anything, she could not abide any form of sexism or racism.

My mother was deeply moved by the oppression she witnessed as a young woman. She was attracted to the satyagraha struggles of Mahatma Gandhi. From the age of nineteen years she became active in resistance politics, supporting the continuous struggles of the Indian community in Transvaal against a government intent on limiting the freedoms of that community. The continuous legislative onslaught of successive South African governments meant that people of Indian descent were increasingly restricted in terms of where they could work, trade and live. In her political activism my mother exemplified the selflessness and the dedication that was so evident among members of our movement during that period.

As I look back on my mother's life I realise just how selflessly she dedicated her life to furthering the aims of justice and democracy at great personal cost. As a cadre of the struggle she never flinched when duty called. She was a courageous woman dedicated to the cause of justice, democracy and equality for all. My mother was active in resistance politics from at least 1937 onwards. Even while she was pregnant with my brother Essop, she went to demonstrate against the oppression and injustice. And all through her years she never sought positions in the movement. She was selfless in the pursuit of our country's national liberation.

For me what truly epitomises my mother and her unique contribution was captured by President Mandela who, in *Long Walk to Freedom*, describes the effect of 'this charming woman' who went to jail for her beliefs. He writes: 'If I had once questioned the willingness of the Indian community to protest against oppression, I no longer could.' In a similar vein, Tata Sisulu noted that he initially had thought Indian women were 'conservative and unwilling to involve themselves in public life'. That changed after he had met my mother and she, along with other Indian women, inspired him with their involvement in the Passive Resistance Campaign. In her very being, in every fibre of her soul, my mother believed in and practised non-racialism.

She ensured that our house was a haven for all those engaged in the struggle against apartheid. Many of the leaders of the Congress Alliance, including Nelson Mandela, Walter Sisulu, Ahmed Kathrada, Dr Dadoo and others frequented our home, and my mother made sure that all who came to the door were well received, treated with dignity and accorded full respect. Albertina and Walter Sisulu, in their biography, said that Goolam and Amina Pahad at Orient House provided '… a home away from home at the City Centre'. Without a doubt, my mother created an environment at Orient House where people from all walks of life were welcomed and where politics was actively deliberated and debated. Such was the atmosphere she created that my brothers and I through osmosis absorbed a set of values and an ethos that led us naturally along the path of political commitment to a set of ideals enshrined in the Freedom Charter. At our home in London, while we were in exile, my mother replicated the open-house policy of our flat in Orient House. And my mother did this unobtrusively but with immense effectiveness.

When, after the Second World War, the Smuts government threatened to pass the Asiatic Land Tenure Act to restrict the occupation and ownership land rights of the Indian community drastically, the South African Indian Congress (SAIC) launched a concerted protest action in which my mother was fully involved. After the Smuts government passed this act in 1946, the South African Indian Congress decided to embark on a passive resistance campaign to head off the challenge. In Durban the Congress called on volunteers to occupy a plot of land reserved for whites only, thus directly defying the unjust law. Though passive, it was known that this action would be dangerous because of the imminent threat of violence from right-wingers and government supporters, let alone reactive action from the state.

My mother was amongst the first to volunteer. While at first the police did not take any direct action against the defiance volunteers, they permitted gangs of white hooligans to attack the volunteers while they looked on. My mother was among those injured and who received medical attention. Despite the injury and goading of the attackers, my mother's spirit remained undampened and she returned to resist again and again. She, along with other resisters, was eventually arrested, tried and summarily sentenced to a fine or imprisonment. All the resisters refused to pay and served their time in prison. Despite having five young children, my mother persisted in her support of the campaign and courted imprisonment for the second time.

Indeed the example set by resisters like my mother in the 1946 Passive Resistance Campaign was of great significance in re-affirming the nobility of adopting passive resistance as a form of protest and the following year served as the basis on which a working relationship was established between the SAIC and the African National Congress. A pact was signed between these organisations in terms of which they would support each other.

In 1952, the ANC and the SAIC jointly launched the Defiance Campaign against six targeted unjust and racist laws. When volunteers were called for, my mother was once again amongst them. Now suffering from rheumatism developed during her earlier bouts in prison, she left behind her children to participate in the Defiance Campaign. Later, my mother would take part in the Women's March to the Union Buildings to protest against the extension of apartheid legislation to black women in urban areas in 1956.

My mother was a woman committed to the struggle against apartheid. She combined her responsibilities as a woman, a freedom fighter and a mother in a fashion that exemplified the best traditions of women's emancipation and liberation in our country. Through her efforts I became part of a much larger family – the family of the Congress Alliance and a family embedded in the broader community of which we were all an integral part. Though our home was intensely political, family and friends, young and old, were always welcome. My mother made no distinction between blood relatives and the broader community – she taught me that we were all part of one big family simply by virtue of being human and by virtue of our common aspirations.

As I remember my mother, despite her lack of fluency in English, interacting with leaders of the Congress Alliance, with members of the community and with each and every one of us, I am humbled by the recognition that she is the role model I have always sought to emulate. My mother was more than a suffragette seeking the right to vote. She championed emancipation and empowerment, human rights and national liberation, and through her actions, her dedication and the way she treated everyone, she quietly and in her own way influenced a generation of Congress leaders.

I am certain my mother would be proud and immensely happy that her dedication to social justice and national liberation rubbed off on me and my other siblings. Today my eldest brother, Dr Essop Pahad, is minister in the presidency of South Africa. My youngest brother, Mr Zunaid Pahad, is a City Councillor in Johannesburg. My other surviving brother, Mr Naseem Pahad, is a successful businessman. It is a great tragedy that my mother, who died in a car accident in India on 26 May 1973, did not live to see freedom in her lifetime. She would have smiled a hugely satisfied smile in 1994 when South Africa attained freedom and democracy took root in our country, and she would have reminded us all that this was only the beginning and that much more needed to be accomplished.

Aziz Pahad was born in Schweizer-Reneke in North West. In 1963, under the apartheid regime, he was given a banning order. In 1966 he left South Africa and lived mostly in London (where he studied International Relations at the University College of London and University of Sussex) but also spent time in Angola and Zimbabwe. In 1991, a year after returning from exile, he was appointed deputy head of the ANC's Department of International Affairs. In 1994 he was appointed deputy minister of foreign affairs in the government of President Nelson Mandela, a position which he still holds.

Lucas Radebe

'WHAT ABOUT YOUR EDUCATION?'

Emily Tlaleng Radebe, born 6 August 1940 in
Magaliesburg

I come from a sporting family. Everybody is involved in sport because of my mom. I was the one playing serious football in the family but all my eleven brothers and sisters were athletes, footballers, netballers – everybody because of her. She used to take us to the local football grounds to watch my older brother play and she supported the local team. In our family she was the only one who supported Kaizer Chiefs; everybody else supported Orlando Pirates.

My mom is very special. She was the one who looked after us because my dad was always away. He was involved in transport so he was always in Rustenburg. That's why we are so many – we are six brothers and five sisters at home. Whenever he came home there was a baby and then he would be gone for a month again and then he would be back. So we got attached to our mom. She was the one who was doing everything for us. I think that's the reason why I am who I am today. It is because of her. You know moms, they want the best for the kids and my mom was always saying, 'I want you to be a doctor!'

My mom suffered and struggled a lot when she was young. She got married when she was sixteen or seventeen to my dad. She always worked at home, cleaned the house, cooked. She is a very strong woman.

All thirteen of us lived in a four-roomed house when I grew up. It had two bedrooms, a kitchen and a den. We were scraping by. When my dad was away and we did not have money my mom used to run a crèche for the kids of the neighbours and of our community. You would come home and the house would be full of children. Everybody was welcome.

She owned a spaza shop, all to pull us through. She sold bread and more. She was involved in the community, lead a choir and she even used to spend her money on assisting the team to travel or for the choir. Even now she has a netball team and a football team, and she insists on running them herself.

The reason I went to North West was because of her. She wanted me to be a doctor – that's what she said. People who earned money and got good jobs were doctors and lawyers. During the time of violence in Soweto I remember when my brother went to school in Bophuthatswana. She sent me there too to get away from Soweto, and I went there purely for educational purposes. I was fifteen years old. The school was very strict – school was serious business. Bophuthatswana was very rural, and the school was in a place called Lehurtshe, in the middle of nowhere. I was getting bored and I joined one of the clubs. I started training with them during the day, after I had finished my home-work. However, my mother would check up on me. She said: 'You can play ball, but school first,' and she was constantly communicating with the principal: 'How is he doing? Is he doing okay? If he does not do his school work, call me!'

So in the late eighties, around 1989, I was playing football. I was really good and I remember somebody from Kaizer Chiefs saying, 'If you are interested, we want you to come to Jo'burg to come and train and see if you're good enough to join the club.' I replied: 'Ask my mom!'

Kaizer Chiefs was a big club. My mom asked: 'You want to play foot-ball? Which team? Kaizer Chiefs? The Glamour Boys? It's an excuse to have parties, to run around. No, finish your school first!' So I was not allowed to go. They came back to me and said: 'Your mom is not happy but we want you. Can't you just come here, just for the weekend, so that we can see?'

'If my mom said no then I can't!' I replied. But they insisted. Eventually I rang my mom and asked: 'Mom, please let me try, I will only go there for the weekend and then I'll go back.' And I went and I was good – they were very impressed. I went straight back to school because my mom did not want to see me in Jo'burg, in Soweto. But the club came back and said, We are very impressed, we want to sign you up. I said: 'Ask my mom!' My mom said: 'This is a huge decision. You have to decide, either you stay there in school or you come here. But if you come here, I don't want to hear stories. You go to school. If you continue your education and they put you through college then you can play, that's my view.' I was about nineteen or twenty then.

So I signed with the big club Kaizer Chiefs and I started to play well. In my first year we played in a Cup and I was named Player of the Series. That was brilliant! My friends and the neighbours were excited because I was playing for a professional soccer team, but my mother reminded me: 'What about school?'

They actually promised to get me into one of the colleges. When I left Bophuthatswana I had finished my matric and I was attending the College of Education. It was the first day of the college – they only opened that year in 1990. When I left, I came to Jo'burg, signed and started playing for Kaizer Chiefs.

I did very, very well. And I remember that I redid the house for my mom with my first salary. I knew how we had grown up and I knew where my mom and us had come from. I promised her that this was what I wanted to do with my first salary! There were a lot of us for a four-roomed house; we extended the house, made it a three-bedroomed house with a kitchen, TV lounge and dining room. She needed the third room for the boys. 'The boys must get out of the house, sleep outside,' she said.

Later when I bought my first car, she went with me. I remember I had said that I was earning money now and that I wanted a car. She asked: 'Who is going to drive the car, you don't have a licence? How can you drive a car?'

'Can't I just go and buy myself a car?' I asked.

'Let's go, I am coming with you!' she said and went with me to buy my first car.

When we got the car she asked who was driving the car back home: 'You do not have a licence.' I was so careful driving the car home. 'The car stays here until you get your licence,' she said. I promised to get a licence. So I got my licence. But when I went out with the car she never went to sleep until I was home. Never ever! I could come home at four in the morning and while I would be opening the gate, she would be opening the door. She shouted but she was very sweet.

One time she told my dad to take off the wheels of the car and put them on top of the garage so that I couldn't leave, because she wanted me to stay home until I finished school and not go out at night to parties. After three years playing for Kaizer Chiefs, she was still asking, 'What about your education?'

Then after Chiefs, Leeds United came. I again had to ask my mom, but my dad was on my side. 'Let him go!' he said. I did not know what to expect. I did not know England but I went and played football in England. My parents came to visit. That was nice, I was really proud of my parents, especially my mom. It was wonderful to invite them to stay with me in Leeds.

So I lived in Leeds, a good life, and she and my dad used to visit often. When I got involved in football in Leeds I was introduced to charity work, which really changed my life. I realised that I was taking after my mom. She used to give – she would give you her last cent. She was very generous, she *is* very generous, and today she is giving away my money. I ask her, 'How can you take my money and give it to somebody else?' But I soon started to look at life from a different angle. I looked back and realised where I had come from, the house in the township where we had grown up. I still go there.

Yes, I played the sport, I enjoyed the game, I made a career out of the game and my mom was proud of me, but there was one thing she still wanted from me: 'I want you to be a doctor!'

After I had retired, I was invited back to Leeds. I had been in the UK for twelve years and played football for eleven years for one team. For this they honoured me by giving me a testimonial before my last football match. The stadium was packed, my parents were there, I was so proud. I had a gala dinner and gave the proceeds to charity. I worked with SOS Children's Village, the Reach for a Dream Foundation, the Starfish Foundation, local charities in Leeds and the Leeds General Hospital.

It was sad that I was leaving. I went back to South Africa and did the same there: had my last football match and took my parents. Everybody came to watch the game. They had a hospitality suite named after me, the Lucas Radebe suite. They were singing my name. It made me very proud.

Football taught me a lot of things. With the game came responsibility. Wearing that surname on my back gave me goosebumps every weekend. I knew that I was representing my friends in the townships, representing my parents and representing my country, whether it was with Leeds or with Bafana Bafana. I was ever so proud of that.

Football taught me that life is not only about yourself, it is about all the other people who are around you. It is about the people who like you *and* the people who hate you, especially those who hate you, because you want to prove them wrong and you always do your best to prove them wrong. So this means that even the ones who don't like you develop your football and make you perform at your best – a good thing because not everybody will like you.

And also, don't forget where you came from. I used to go to school without a lunch box: I would drink tea and eat bread in the morning, go to school, run home at lunch time, drink tea and bread, go back to school. At night, I would have porridge and milk, sometimes go to bed without food, sometimes only eat once or twice a day. I will never forget that and I will remember that there are people who are worse off than that today, some lying in hospitals they cannot afford. Now that I can afford it, I want to show them that they are not alone. I always wanted to share. And I love my charity work. I think a lot of this is because of my mom. I also always give my family what they need, just to make sure that they're looked after.

In 2005 something great happened. Now that I have become old, I was invited to Leeds and honoured by Leeds University. They gave me a degree, an honorary doctorate. I asked them, 'How much is the gown? I am buying the gown.'

'No, you can take the gown, you can take everything!' they replied.

'I am going home like this to my mom,' I said.

I flew back from Leeds with the gown and went straight to my mom. 'Do you remember what you said about football? I asked. 'Look, Mom, there is the certificate and everything, I am a doctor now!'

You should have seen my smile! It could light up this room. She was so proud, there was nothing more satisfying than that.

Not understanding what an honorary doctorate means, she said, 'Now the kids will not suffer from disease, and you can help …'

Today my parents are both retired and my mom still has a house full of children. She keeps me going and has taught me to appreciate life!

Lucas Radebe was born in the Diepkloof section of Soweto as one of eleven children. He is a former Leeds United and South African football player. He earned 70 'caps' for South Africa. At the end of the 2005 season, he retired from professional football and became involved in charity work. He has been an ambassador of FIFA for SOS Children's Villages and received the FIFA Fair Play Award in December 2000 for his contribution to ridding soccer of racism as well as for his work with children in South Africa.

Albie Sachs

REVOLUTIONARY TYPIST

Ray Edwards, born Rachel Ginsburg, formerly
Ray Sachs. Born 1905 near Vilna, Lithuania,
came to Pretoria in 1906 as a babe in arms.
Died 1998 in Cape Town

One of my very first memories is of walking on the beach at Clifton after being told 'Your father's coming,' and seeing big white tennis shoes. My father and mother were separated at the time. I looked up … up … up and way above me was a head and a body talking to me. Solly Sachs, my dad, was a trade union leader, a warm, passionate and highly effective organiser, and very controversial. At his funeral in 1976 in London, one of the speakers said, 'and I'm quite sure if God exists, Solly's up there arguing with him right now.'

But it was my mother, Ray, soft-spoken, always a conciliator, who was to have the biggest influence on my life. She would be the one to type up the political resolutions while the men comrades were playing cards after a busy day in the struggle. Unduly modest about her own abilities, but totally committed to the cause of human liberation, she was always working, getting things done, and looking after two little kids. And surrounded by people who were strong personalities, vivacious, interesting, laughing, many of them women on their own, sometimes with children, sometimes without. I didn't have an option – I grew up a troublemaker who was a natural feminist.

I also grew up spontaneously anti-racist. Ideas and values counted for everything, possessions for very little. My mom worked as a typist for Moses Kotane, a prominent leader in the African National Congress and general secretary of the South African Communist Party. She had taught him at night school and he used to say, 'Well, Ray taught me to read and write and now I'm her boss!' My mom would always tell me and my brother to tidy up before Uncle Moses arrived. My first years were spent in an atmosphere where it was absolutely normal for a white woman to be working for an African man and to have special respect for him.

I don't recall getting didactic lessons from either her or my dad, and hated them for assuming I would automatically agree with their views just because I was their son. But it was the example they set and the things that they regarded as important that prepared me, wonderfully, it turned out, for a turbulent life where fables came to be true.

And here is a tribute I wrote to my mom:

For me, the twentieth century ended when my mother died in her ninety-second year. She had been born at the same time of the 1905 Revolution in Russia, had come as a baby to Pretoria, and had embraced much of the passion and drama of the globe through her involvement, from adolescence to old age, in the struggle for human dignity and social justice in South Africa. Though eventually blind and unable to care for herself physically, her mind and humor remained spirited until the end. She had been elated when her elderly and frail neighbours in Highlands House had congratulated her on her son the lawyer being made a judge, just as she had been deeply proud of the achievements of her son the doctor who had become a distinguished medical scientist. She had loved the occasional visits from members of the ANC Women's League who had kept her informed of their activities. The one thing she had insisted on during our last visits was that she not be buried or cremated, but that her body be donated to Medical School. After she died, I learned that getting into Medical School was not easy, not even when you were dead. The official concerned indicated that there would have to be an examination: the body could not be too obese, death must not have resulted from an infectious disease, and the body should not have been subject to trauma – could I return the next day? Twenty four hours later I went back with some anxiety to the mortuary to get the news: it was good, my mother had passed! Goodbye, Mommy, revolutionary typist, you never lost your desire to be helpful nor your spirit of personal self-determination, you led a long and honourable life, and you contributed much to the new South Africa. I feel proud to have been your son and to have lived much of my life according to your emancipatory values, the noblest of this brilliant and tortured century.

From *The Soft Vengeance of a Freedom Fighter*

Albie Sachs grew up in Clifton, Cape Town. He was appointed to the court by Nelson Mandela in 1994 and is a justice of the Constitutional Court of South Africa. He is also a writer and won the Alan Paton Award for his book *The Soft Vengeance of a Freedom Fighter* in 1991.

Tina Schouw

LOVE IS HIDDEN IN
UNCONVENTIONAL PLACES

Sylvestra Abbelga, born 31 December 1910 in
Cape Town, died 10 March 1993 in Cape Town

My great-grandfather, Zacharius Abbelgas, was a Pilipino fisherman from Cebu, Manila, who had wanderlust. He made his way to Cape Town on a fishing trawler and at the harbour he promptly jumped ship, determined to make a new life for himself in South Africa. It was in Kalk Bay that he met and fell in love with a beautiful, exotic woman, my great-grandmother Elizabeth … They married and had seven children – Spirion, Elias, Pedro, Lorenzo, Crisenciana and twin daughters Sylvestra and Annastacia.

My grandmother was Sylvestra Abbelgas. She was a short, dark, handsome woman with laughing eyes and thick, straight, jet-black hair, the telltale sign of her Pilipino descent of which she was very proud. This energetic and feisty woman took care of me and many cousins from the ages of five to six whilst our mothers worked.

I recall my mother dropping me off at her house one day and I started to cry. But 'Ma' (that's what we called her) stopped the tears in their tracks with her no-nonsense attitude by saying, 'Come, Tina, no crying, your mommy's going to work now, but you'll see her later. Say goodbye.' Then she bent down, gave me a rough kiss on the cheek and bundled me unceremoniously into the house. And that was that. No long, reassuring hugs or comforting cuddles to ease my separation anxieties. It was not in her nature to do so. Yet I felt safe in her home at Number 61 Goldsmith Road, Salt River. The world seemed to operate around the axis that was her home, and for that short period it was the world to me.

Her kitchen was huge and inviting, a haven to those in need. Here she conjured up her favourite mouth-watering dishes of bean curry and tripe and trotters. I loved the strange texture of the tripe on my tongue and the sticky glutinous goo of the trotters that tasted so much better licked off my fingers. I can smell the odours wafting from the kitchen like an aromatic genie that magically enticed friends and family from afar to drop in for a surprise visit. Welcomed guests often came into the kitchen saying, 'Aunty Sylvestra, that smells so good, can I have some?' And on cue a dish was hauled out of the cupboard, a ladle whisked from the drawer and a generous helping of hot food was served into a bowl and handed to the eager hands. And whilst they ate, there was the familiar smell of Ceylon tea brewing, whistling on the boil, ready for pouring into the open mouths of the elaborately patterned floral cups and saucers.

This wicked combination of home-cooked food and comforting tea made with practical necessity would unleash a sea of emotions from the unsuspecting guest. And suddenly, into the ample arms of the kitchen, laughter and tears like a pent-up dam would burst forth and gush out onto the kitchen table, where Ma and the warm rays of the sun filtering through the kitchen window would be ready to receive them.

I can hear her firm voice shooing me out of the kitchen to go and play on the *stoep* so that she could commiserate with a friend, offer sound advice or laugh at some ridiculous situation that was not meant for innocent ears. And when all burdens were laid down and put to rest she would send off the heartened guest with food parcels and old clothes for younger siblings. Her kitchen like her heart was a soft place to fall.

Taking care of us, doing household chores and dressmaking meant that her time was limited, and often she was rushed off her feet. One day I went into town with her on some errands. First to the material stalls at the Grand Parade to stock up on some fine fabric and cotton and then to buy some dried fruit and nuts from Wellingtons in Darling Street. I struggled to keep up with her short, quick steps, but I quickly learnt to keep pace, for there really was no other option.

The promised treat of a cream doughnut to savour on the bus on the way back home was the light at the end of the tunnel and she never failed in this regard. Just like she never failed to put shiny, silver fifty-cent pieces into her fruity Christmas puddings served with thick yellow custard, which made me eat my dessert even faster in the hope of finding the buried treasures.

But more than anything else I love the recollection of the late after-noons we spent together, when the cooking was done, the customers fitted, the kids fed and the household chores finished. It was then that she would slow down, take a break and say, 'Get your dancing shoes.' And we'd be off in a flash to my aunt's room and return with her big ballet shoes on our small feet. Then we'd take our positions and she would clap her hands and sing, la lala lala laala laala to the melody of 'Glow Little Glow-Worm' whilst we twirled like whirling dervishes with such delight to her exuberant accompaniment. I recall this memory with such fondness, for it was moments like these that grew the young girl child that was me. And whilst we danced and sang along with her she smiled, oh how she smiled.

Ma was not your typical grandmother who used gentle encouraging words to comfort me or gave sweet loving embraces. Her manner sometimes appeared brusque and awkward and often I got the distinct impression that she was uncomfortable with showing affection, even though she always welcomed me with a smile. And so I found myself asking the question, 'Did she love me?' My reply is that her love was hidden, but that it was present.

It was there in her practical commitment to care for me and my cousins, whilst juggling so many other balls. It was there in her common sense and unsentimental approach to life that said, Just do the best you can. It was present in the rough, clumsy kisses on my cheek that encouraged me to let go and move on. It was nestled in the gooey mixture of her Christmas pudding that taught me sometimes you have to wade through life's stickiness to find its hidden treasures. It was there in the special time she set aside daily to wing my creativity.

I am following her lead by keeping with the tradition of nurturing my spirit and feeding my soul. It was affirmed in the echo of her singing and the clapping of her hands, and now I sing and write the songs my soul has learnt to grow. She made me aware that as an artist I need to nurture my dreams, shine my light on them and grow the wings to fly. This year I have birthed twin dreams that are now a reality. One being a CD called *The Goodnight Songs* and the other an inspirational children's book called *Dreamwalking*. I can hear her singing her appraisal and affirming me with her song, 'Glow Little Glow-Worm'.

And so with common sense and practical know-how inherited from my grandmother and my gift of intuition, pursuing my dreams comes naturally now and I am learning how to shine. But sometimes when life's pace gets too fast and I feel myself going under, I slow down and take time out. And then, like magic from out of the blue, a dogged determination married with a feisty spirit kicks in just like Ma's, and once again I find myself in full swing, walking my dreams.

Ma taught me that loving is in the doing, and her example of helping yourself and others in so many different ways has guided me to do the same. I know for certain that love comes in many forms and often not in ways you expect. I've learnt that sometimes love is unconventional. And that is okay. I've learnt that just because the words 'I love you' are not said, it doesn't mean that love is missing. I've learnt to look carefully and find it in hidden places.

As the mother of my five-year-old son Mika, I juggle care-giving, household chores and a career like mothers everywhere. Some days I am flying and other days I feel as though I am getting it all horribly wrong. But then I think about Ma and somehow I know that everything will be fine. And yes, she was not the perfect grandmother, but to me she was perfect, she was enough. I know for sure that nobody gets it perfectly right. I am learning to take everything step by step and I realise that being in the moment and doing the best I can is all I can ask of myself.

My wish for my son is that he will learn how to recognise love hidden in unconventional places and that he will know that his true nature is to glow. And so, with certainty I know that as I stand in my truth with my grandmother at my side, I am glowing, I am perfect and I am enough.

Tina Schouw is a singer, songwriter, musician and actress. She was born in Cape Town. From 1987 to 1989 she was invited by anti-apartheid organisations to perform solo shows in Holland, Germany and Switzerland. She returned to South Africa in 1990 and over the past ten years has been performing her original material and jazz in all the top musical venues in Cape Town.

Ayanda Sisulu

MY GOGO

Albertina Nontsikelelo Sisulu, born 21 October
1918 in the Tsomo district of the Transkei

Albertina Sisulu is my maternal grandmother. She is known to many
South Africans as Mama Sisulu or Mama. My granddad used to call her
Tini (short for Albertina). My granny is a well known figure in South Africa,
having been the wife of an ANC stalwart. She is a substantial historical
figure in her own right, of course. She was a founding member of the
ANC Women's League. She was instrumental in organising the famous
Women's March in 1956 to the Union Buildings in Pretoria, where more
than twenty thousand women protested against the repressive pass laws.
She was the first woman to be arrested under the apartheid ninety-day
detention law that allowed for imprisonment without trial. A lot has
been written about her and I therefore find it a rather intimidating task to
write about her here. Having mulled it over for a while I figured the best
thing to do would be to share some of my most memorable moments
with her.

I lived with my granny from the time I was born until I was about
three years old. My mother was imprisoned in the student uprising of
1976 and I was left in the care of my granny and my youngest aunt,
Nkuli. When I was about two years old my granny was making supper
and I was rushing around the kitchen, playing on the floor. At some
point my granny moved a pan of boiling gravy from the stove and placed
it on the counter as she prepared to dish up the food. Having refused
to be kicked out of the kitchen where I was making a right nuisance of
myself, I thought I would pacify her by being helpful. So I reached up to
grasp the pan of gravy, pulling down the handle and bringing down the
hot gravy all over my chest.

I remember very little of what happened immediately afterwards, but I am pretty sure that it was total chaos. After that I delighted in telling anybody who would listen that 'uGogo ungishile!' ('Gogo burnt me!'), while dramatically revealing my scarred chest. My poor granny endured many disapproving looks as a result, but she never scolded me for it. I am happy to say that after thirty years all I have left in terms of a scar is a small light patch, one centimetre in diameter.

My grandparents were married in 1944, the same year that the ANC Youth League was formed. My granddad was sentenced to life imprisonment on 12 June 1964 after the Rivonia Trial. When I was born my granddad had already been in prison for twelve years. My first memory of my granddad was when we went to visit him at Pollsmoor Prison. I think I was about five years old. I had also been to Robben Island as a baby, but have no memory of it. My granny was very excited at the prospect of the upcoming visit and even had her teeth polished.

We took the midnight flight to Cape Town. This was my first time on a plane. It was so exciting! My granny let me sit in the aisle seat so I could watch in awe as the hostess handed out (free!) tea and small chocolates. My granny gave me hers. I was in heaven. Visits to Cape Town were very expensive and in order to visit my granddad we had to apply for permission, which wasn't always granted. Therefore visits to my granddad were very precious and anticipated even more than Christmas.

I remember when we arrived at the prison, a hugely intimidating grey building. We were not allowed contact visits at that point and my granny and I had to speak to my granddad through a thick glass pane. I don't quite remember if there was a phone or a hole in the middle of the glass. My granny chatted away happily and all I could do was sit quietly next to her and bite my lip, willing myself not to cry. I didn't fully understand what was going on, but I felt a deep sense of sadness. My granny was very quiet on the drive back to the guesthouse where we were staying. She never cried, though, which I did for most of the journey.

The happiest I have ever seen my granny was when my granddad was finally released from prison. She looked like a newlywed, beaming and smiling from ear to ear. I cannot imagine what she was feeling, but she looked completely radiant. Her life was turned upside down immediately and she had to deal with constant visitors to the house, media attention and endless functions. She rarely complained about having to share her husband – she was so proud of him and elated to have him back.

In January 2008 the family was devastated by the loss of the eldest of the grandchildren, Mlungisi Sisulu, Jr. (Lungi). As we were preparing for the funeral, I was sifting through old photos to make a video collage of Lungi's life. I came across a photo of my granny and granddad with Lungi in the kitchen of their Orlando West house in Soweto. In the photo Lungi is sharing a joke with my granddad and they are both laughing hard, heads thrown back. My granny is in the background with a pot in one hand and a dishing-up spoon in the other. She is smiling and is looking on, contentedly. That is how I remember the early days following my granddad's release from prison. A simple red brick house in the middle of the township, the same house the family had lived in before my granddad had been imprisoned. A home full of love and laughter. That was when my granny was at her happiest, just being a wife, mother and grandmother.

My granny was born and raised in a village in the then Transkei. When she married my granddad her village upbringing came to good use as their home became a meeting point for ANC activists at the time. She always made sure there were refreshments readily available.

My grandparents had five children of their own and adopted four more. The last time I counted, my granny had twenty-one grandchildren and nine great-grandchildren. Growing up, I used to ask my mom what it felt like being part of such a big family (I was an only child for nine years) and if she ever suffered from 'middle child syndrome'. She would always answer that the one thing her mom had made very clear was that there were to be no favouritism. My grandmother made no distinction between her biological children and the others. And now, being one of almost two dozen grandchildren, I still feel very special whenever I see her. I recently received a phone call from my cousin Vuvu who lives with my granny. Vuvu said that Gogo was complaining that she hadn't seen me in a while and asked when I would be bringing the baby for a visit. I don't know how she does it. My own mother often calls me by either my little brother or sister's name, and there are only four of us!

In 1994, when Nelson Mandela was elected the first black president of South Africa, my granny was elected to the South African Parliament. She was given the honour of nominating Nelson Mandela for president of South Africa in the National Assembly. What made her most proud, however, was that she was elected to Parliament along with two of her children – my mom, Lindiwe, and my uncle Max. She was absolutely delighted to tell people that the family who had the most members in Parliament was the Sisulus and that she was the only mother who had two children in Parliament!

My granny was one of the first visitors I had in hospital after my daughter Aamani was born. Aamani was a day old when she got to meet her great-granny. At that stage, I was totally exhausted and over-whelmed after my first night as a mom. Aamani was refusing to latch on and I was stressed. When my granny arrived with my mom, aunt Zodwa and cousin Vuvu in tow, Aamani was in the nursery and I was napping. Of course my granny quickly dispatched a nurse to bring the baby into the room. Aamani arrived, still fast asleep. Having been passed around and undressed to be checked for ten fingers and ten toes, she woke up. And wailed! Loudly! My granny, a nurse by training and experienced mother, grandmother and great-grandmother instructed me to feed her. 'Feed her!' she exclaimed rather impatiently, 'She's hungry.'

My protestations that she had been fed an hour before were met with such a disapproving look that I gave in and attempted to do the impossible: feed my newborn, which I didn't manage to do. After a few minutes of stressed attempts, I gave up and called for the nurse to bring a bottle of formula. My granny tut-tutted and I wished the ground would open up and swallow me!

While I have many very happy memories of my granny I also have some incredibly painful ones. The worst was when my granddad passed away. I had been settling down to watch *Law & Order* on TV when I got a call from Vuvu that my granddad had stopped breathing. I immediately rushed over to the house (I lived about ten minutes away). I was the first family member to arrive after the paramedics. As I walked down the passage towards my grandparents' bedroom, terrified at the sight of all the paramedics visible through the doorway, I came across my granny on the floor of the spare bedroom. She was lying in a crumpled heap on the floor, repeatedly wailing in Xhosa: 'What am I without him?' At that point I knew my granddad had left us.

My attempts to coax her off the floor and onto the bed were futile. I was struck by the enormity of the situation. She had just lost the love of her life whom she had only gotten back after almost three decades in jail. There was nothing I could say or do to make things better. Eventually I managed to get a pillow in between her head and the floor and then crouched next to her and cradled her.

I was very relieved when Ma Tambo arrived after what must have been thirty minutes, although it felt like an eternity. Ma Tambo was infinitely more qualified to deal with the situation, having herself lost her husband a few years before. She managed to get my granny onto the bed. More family members arrived at the house well into the night. My granny cried for several more hours and was eventually sedated. On the day of the funeral, almost two weeks later, my granny hardly shed a tear. Everyone remarked how brave she was. Little did they know that she just had no more tears left. She was completely cried out by then.

In 2007, the Gauteng Provincial Government named the R21/R24 highway in Johannesburg the Albertina Sisulu Freeway to honour my granny. When Gauteng Premier Mbhazima Shilowa announced the renaming of the highway, he said the intention was to honour and acknowledge Mama Sisulu for her contribution to the liberation of this country, the building of democracy and women's emancipation. When searching for a new name for the highway, the Gauteng Executive was looking for a name that would reflect the values and principles of justice, equality, ethical conduct and, above all, unity.

I feel very blessed to have had my granny as a role model, and to have had her in my life for so long. I can only hope that when I've grown up (I am only thirty-two!) my own grandchildren will look back at my small contribution and be even a tiny bit as proud of me as I am of my own granny, my gogo, Albertina Nontsikelelo Sisulu.

Ayanda Xoliswa Sisulu, granddaughter of Albertina and Walter Sisulu, completed her honours degree at Wetherley College in the United States and gained extensive experience in the investment banking industry. In 2005 she was appointed Business Development Director: Business Development for Rand Merchant Bank.

Gillian Slovo

TWO 'FIRST' LADIES AHEAD
OF THEIR TIME

Mathilda (Tilly) First, 1898(?)–1992, born
in Johannesburg, died in Johannesburg;
Ruth First (née First), 1925–1982, born in
Johannesburg, died in Maputo (pictured)

My grandmother Tilly First left school at thirteen. Her career was not supposed to be important. She was only a girl who was born in the dying days of the nineteenth century. Her life's aspiration must therefore, conventional wisdom dictated, be to marry and have children. But first, it fell to her, the daughter of impoverished immigrants, to earn the money to put her brother through his accountancy course. So she would get up early to iron her brother's shirts and make his lunch and then she would go out to work, at first in a shoe shop and later in a place that sold furniture on hire purchase to poor white miners.

This job was what politicised her. In 1922 the miners went on strike. It was partly a racist strike – the white miners were trying to stop the mine owners from putting Africans into some 'white' jobs. But when Tilly saw how her boss repossessed miners' furniture as soon as they failed to make a weekly payment (and this despite the fact that he must have known that, as soon the strike was over, the miners would repay him) her eyes were opened. She began to understand how hard ordinary people worked and how little they gained from it. Thus began her journey into radicalism.

She was an amazing woman, my grandmother. Her own mother had only ever spoken Yiddish – but by the time I came onto the scene, Tilly had the accent not of a white South African but of a British queen. She was a woman who, with only one kidney, lived into her nineties. She was also someone who, although she never got to finish school, used to respond to my boasts of the novels and history books from the 1940s and 1950s I was reading with a curt: 'Oh yes. I remember that one. I read it when it first came out.' She was a hard woman to have as a mother, I think: she could be cold and she could be judgemental. She was a stiff taskmaster, difficult to satisfy. And my mother Ruth was her beloved daughter.

There's a story Tilly used to tell about Ruth. Ruth was about seventeen, Tilly said, when she had climbed the Johannesburg City Hall steps to give her first public speech. It must have been mid-War, around 1942. The Party used to hold rallies on the steps, arguing for change, and these rallies were often also the target of Brown Shirt (fascist) violence. And there was Ruth, in this fevered and frightening atmosphere, aged seventeen, delivering a passionate speech.

Having set this scene, Tilly would then describe how, after Ruth had finished, a comrade had congratulated Tilly on how well her young daughter had done. In reply, Tilly had enumerated the ways in which Ruth could have improved her performance.

I think there was a double purpose to this story. It was Tilly's way of indirectly expressing pride in her daughter (a kind of 'As long as I'm critical, I can also boast about how wonderful Ruth is') but it also pointed to an aspect of Tilly's character and of her aspirations that were not fulfilled.

Tilly felt passionately about politics and about the evils of racism, and yet her own position was always secondary to her equally radical husband's. So much so that when she first tried to join the Communist Party she was rejected on the grounds of her husband being a capitalist (and this was by that same capitalist Julius who was actually treasurer of the Communist Party). Tilly, because of her brother's needs, had been made to leave school: her daughter Ruth, in contrast, got to go to university. As a young girl Tilly would have wanted badly to achieve what, with her help, her daughter managed.

Tilly was a woman ahead of her time. She would have loved to make her own impact. But because of the era in which she grew up, and especially because of the unequal position of women, she never managed this. All her ambition, all her beliefs, she poured into her daughter – and this included looking after us, her grandchildren, when Ruth was involved in trying to change the world. If Tilly could not make her mark, then Ruth would. And if Ruth was going to do it, Tilly would make sure she did it better than anybody else.

To find their own paths in life, children often need to rebel. But Ruth was born into a family who were already rebels. Many are the funny stories of school friends who, coming home on a play date, were made to sit and listen to Tilly's lecture on the inequities of apartheid and the need for communism. Ruth found her own way of adapting to this. She didn't, as her brother did, decide that politics was her parents' thing. Instead she became an activist in her own right, surpassing Tilly's achievements as only a daughter of Tilly ever could. But she also had a different attitude to politics.

Although her involvement in the movement was her life, Ruth stopped herself and she stopped her husband from talking politics to us, their children. There were external reasons for this restraint – the actions in which they were involved while we were growing up were mostly illegal and not for the ears of or the repeating by children. But a more important reason was that Ruth, who had disliked the manner in which her own mother had indoctrinated her, was opposed to telling children what they should think. She did not want to hand to us a set of ready-made political beliefs. She wanted us to decide for ourselves.

Ruth would never easily swallow a party line. What made her who she was, and what made what she did even more remarkable, was that she always asked questions and always drew her own conclusions. She expected other people to do this as well, and despised those who did not.

Here's how Madiba saw it. In 1975 he wrote to her from Robben Island:

I saw pictures of a woman's indaba in Paris, and the eye was immediately caught by a photo in coat and slacks, resembling a face once
very familiar at cor. Commissioner and Von Nieligh. Bespectacled
and hawk-nosed and with a sheaf of papers as usual, she sat almost
flat on the floor and even looked humble and soft and nearest to
me than she had ever been before. Seeing that picture after so long
evoked pleasant memories and made me forget about her flashes of
temper, impatience and barbed tongue. Does that ring a bell?

It certainly does ring a bell. Anyone who knew Ruth, and this included us, her children, would have occasionally bore the brunt of that same impatience and that same barbed tongue. And they would have stood witness to her sharp mind. For Ruth was quick and she was deep: if she impatiently interrupted people in midstream it was only because she had guessed what they were going to say and was already debating it. It was a quality that could intimidate – especially men. (And dare I say it, perhaps even a man like Madiba?)

This quality sometimes made for difficult interaction between Ruth and her mother. Ruth, the activist, was often annoyed by Tilly's blind faith. Ruth, the daughter who would never let anything, including her own self-doubt, stop her from having a full professional and political life, could be critical of Tilly's disempowered supporting role. And yet in Tilly are the visible seeds of who Ruth became. No accident, perhaps, that they continued to share the same surname, that Ruth, always ahead of her time, insisted on keeping her maiden name in her professional and political life.

Theirs is an amazing story that shows how much they each did to challenge and break with the norms of their society. Ruth, as critical as she might sometimes be of her mother, was in a way a chip off the old block. And what a block it was.

Gillian Slovo is a novelist who lives and works in London. Her 1997 memoir, *Every Secret Thing: My Family, My Country*, is an account of her childhood in South Africa and her relationship with her parents, political activists Joe Slovo and Ruth First. Her 2000 novel, *Red Dust*, explores the meanings and effects of the South African Truth and Reconciliation Commission. In 2004 it was made into a film starring Hilary Swank and Chiwetel Ejiofor. In the same year, her novel *Ice Road* was shortlisted for the Orange Prize and her co-authored play *Guantanamo: 'Honor Bound to Defend Freedom'* was staged in, among other cities, London, Chicago, New York and Washington DC. Her most recent novel, *Black Orchids*, was published in 2008.

Helen Suzman

THREE WOMEN

My mother died when I was born and I had little contact with my two grandmothers when they paid brief visits to their sons who had emigrated from Eastern Europe to South Africa shortly after the Anglo-Boer War. I lived with my father, uncle and aunt together with my older sister for ten years. My aunt was a childless, withdrawn, sad woman who had had five girls, including me and my sister, dumped on her – children of her two deceased sisters. She had little influence on me during the years I lived with her. When I was ten years old, my father remarried and my stepmother, a pleasant woman who loved giving parties, gave my father a life he would never have had otherwise. She taught me about the good things in life and gave me a taste for tailored clothes. She had very little influence, however, on my views in any other way.

Three women who most influenced me were, firstly, Sister Columba, the head nun at Parktown Convent, the school at which I was educated from age ten until I matriculated at seventeen. Sr Columba was a tough, irritable woman who taught me three things apart from excellent English and Latin. Her teaching of history, however, was poor, because it was by rote – ten pages from the history book to be learnt by heart. That certainly gave me a good memory, but I can't say it gave me any insight into what was currently happening in other countries.

Three things she had taught me, however, which I have never forgotten. She used to say in her soft Irish brogue, 'Remember, child, other people's time is as valuable as your own,' and that has made me a very punctual person. It has also made me very irritable with people who keep me waiting! The second important thing I learned from Sr Columba was to be a bad loser. This she instilled in me and my fellow schoolmates by whacking us with a ruler if we had lost a hockey match. We had to win, otherwise we had a whacking from Sr Columba and no buns for tea! The result is, of course, that I am a very bad loser, which was excellent for someone who was destined to be involved in political struggles. I never lost any election I fought for nor the parliamentary seat of Houghton in my thirty-six years as a member of Parliament. Thirdly, she taught me to do things that I didn't wish to do. When such an occasion arises even now, I hear her soft Irish voice saying 'Do it, child' – and I do.

Some thirty years after I had left the convent the phone rang. I picked it up and a voice said, 'Hello, may I speak to Helen please?' And I said, 'Hello, Sr Columba,' and she said, 'Lord love us, child, you remember my voice after all these years.' Well, of course, I could never forget that voice. She told me that all the nuns were praying for my success in the election that I was fighting at that time.

There were two other women who greatly influenced my political convictions. One was Hansi Pollak, a professor at the University of the Witwatersrand, which I attended. She taught me Economic History, and from her I learnt a great deal about the conditions under which black people lived in South Africa and the discriminatory laws that existed during the Smuts regime.

The third woman who influenced me was Dr Ellen Hellman, who was one of the greats at the South African Institute of Race Relations, an organisation devoted to the advancement of liberal democracy. I joined the Institute after the surprise defeat of General Smuts at the end of the Second World War. I did research for the Institute and presented evidence on its behalf to the Fagan Commission – known as the 'Native Laws Commission' – which was set up to investigate and make recommendations for change to the laws applying to black people in urban areas. However, the Smuts government was defeated before any of the recommendations of the Fagan Commission could be implemented. Instead, the apartheid government introduced new discriminatory laws and extended those already in existence.

These three women – Sr Columba, Professor Hansi Pollak and Dr Ellen Hellman – influenced my political allegiance to liberal democracy, which still endures.

Helen Suzman (née Gavronsky) was born in Germiston, Gauteng, as the daughter of Lithuanian–Jewish immigrants. She studied Economics and Statistics at the University of the Witwatersrand and became a lecturer, an anti-apartheid activist and politician. She spent a total of 36 years in Parliament and won world recognition for her ceaseless opposition to the policy of apartheid. She visited Nelson Mandela numerous times in prison and was at his side when he signed the new Constitution in 1996. She died on 1 January 2009.

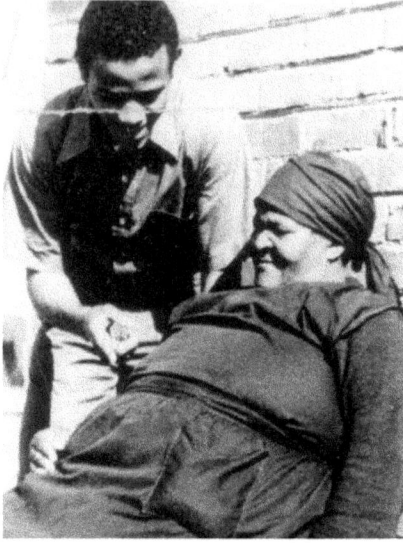

Desmond Tutu

THANK YOU GOD FOR WOMEN,
FOR OUR MOTHERS

Aletta Dorothea (née Mathlare), born
10 April 1904 or 1906 in Boksburg,
died October 1984 in Springs

My earliest and strongest recollection of my mother was of her amazing generosity. I remember as if it were yesterday how she never cooked a meal that would be sufficient just for her family. We were a family of five. My father, Zacheriah, was headmaster of a local primary school wherever we lived. Then there was my mother, Aletta. I had two sisters, one older than I, Sylvia, and the other, younger than I, Gloria. I was an only son, though my mother had given birth to two other boys, one who came after my older sister and the other who would have been our firstborn. Both had died as babies so I was an only one and, in a way, in an African household perhaps, somewhat pampered and spoilt as the son who would ensure that our family name would not disappear and that was important in a patriarchal society. I have noted though that in even seemingly sophisticated societies where the gender of a child is a matter of indifference (really?) a boy child, especially the firstborn boy child, does have a special status not normally accorded girl children. So I was probably, as my sisters have alleged, something of a mommy's favourite and perhaps something of a spoilt brat as a consequence.

But I have digressed. I return to the point I was making about my mother's generosity; that I don't recall her ever cooking a meal just enough for her immediate nuclear family. I know that this was also common practice for many another family. She always had to run the gauntlet of my father's criticism that she was being wasteful for cooking such large meals. But my mother ignored those strictures and continued to expect that someone or someones would pitch up and we should be able to extend the hospitality of a meal to such unexpected guests. And I think this was fairly common knowledge in our neighbourhood for there were those who seemed to know when to pitch up just as Mother was dishing up. Then she would be in her element.

She had not gone beyond elementary school in her education, though she did go to Tigerkloof Institution near Kuruman for a Domestic Science diploma, and in most of her active life she was employed as a domestic worker. And so it was that she was cook at Ezenzeleni Blind Institute near Roodepoort which had been founded by the Reverend Dr Arthur and Mrs Blaxall. My mother cooked for the black blind women. One day when I was perhaps nine years old or so, I recall, in a story I have recounted many times, standing with my mother on the *stoep* of the women's hostel when a white priest in a flowing black cassock swept past and doffed his hat to my mother. This priest was Trevor Huddleston CR. I was quite taken aback – a white man doffing his hat to a black woman and a domestic worker to boot. It left an indelible impression on me. Much later I realised that it was an expression of his theological belief about each one of us being of infinite worth because each one of us is created in the image of God, and that had enormous implications for Christian attitudes to the injustice of racism and was to influence my later ministry and opposition to the iniquity of apartheid.

One of my mother's colleagues at Ezenzeleni was Eskia Mphahlele who had resigned as a teacher because of his opposition to government policies and was working as driver/clerk to Father Blaxall. He was working on his degrees with UNISA. He became the first South African (white or black) to receive an MA in English with distinction from this institution. Of course he went on to become an acclaimed author nominated for the Nobel Prize for Literature. He tried to teach me how to box and we used to run long distances on Saturdays with him to build up our stamina! I don't think I was too apt a student!

We went to live in Munsieville, Krugersdorp, and my mother used to clean and do the washing and ironing for her white madam in town for a daily remuneration of twenty cents, which in those days went much further than even today's twenty rand. I was attending the Johannesburg

Bantu High School in what used to be Western Native Township and through apartheid's madness became Western Coloured Township. During the school week I stayed in a hostel in Sophiatown run by the CR Fathers. On some weekends I would go home to Krugersdorp. I remember so distinctly how at the end of one such weekend there was no money for my fare – neither for the bus to the railway station nor for my train ticket. My mother and I walked to her place of work where her madam paid her her princely wages of twenty cents which she promptly passed on to me to rush to the railway station to catch a train for school. I have never forgotten that my mother that day would get nothing at the end of her working day, that it seemed so like working for nothing. It was so typical of my mother, generous to a fault and so self-sacrificial. Amazing human being. I am so glad she was my mother.

In 1947 I contracted TB and spent twenty months in hospital. They did not have today's effective drugs. Father Huddleston used to visit this township urchin regularly in Rietfontein Hospital near Alexandra Township. And my dear mother would trek all the way from Krugersdorp by train and then catch a bus to Orange Grove and then walk almost three miles from the bus stop to the TB hospital at least once a month. That was a real bind and she did this for nearly two years.

I loved her dearly. My father often drank a lot and sometimes would assault my mother. I would fume, getting really angry with him. I know that had I been physically stronger I would have fought him.

Leah, my wife, called my mother 'the comforter of the afflicted' because she always took the side of whomever was the worst off in an argument. I have told audiences that I resemble my mother physically – short and stumpy, with a large nose. Then I would add that I hope I can resemble her spiritually – to emulate her generosity and compassion and concern for the weak. When I have been asked who the greatest influence has been on me I have without hesitation replied: 'my mother'.

Thank you God for women, for our mothers. Thank you for my mother.

29 January 2008

Desmond M Tutu, Archbishop Emeritus, is a cleric and activist who rose to international fame during the 1980s as an opponent of the apartheid regime. Tutu became the first black South African Anglican archbishop of Cape Town. He chaired the Truth and Reconciliation Commission and is currently the chairman of The Elders. Tutu also campaigns to fight AIDS, poverty and racism. He received the Nobel Peace Prize in 1984.

Pieter-Dirk Uys

REMEMBERING THE
EMPTY SPACE

Helga Bassel, born 2 July 1908
in Berlin, died 26 May 1969 in
Cape Town

Losing a mother is something we all will go through in our lives. But it
was not to be part of my *life*. Her suicide was my introduction to *death*.
By then both my grandmothers had died of old age. That was sad but
inevitable. My stern Afrikaans Ouma Uys and my eccentric Viennese
Oma Bassel communicated with one another carefully in a third language. Their collective broken English was terrible but understandable.
They were great friend against all the odds.

Suicide is different to dying of old age. After that moment nothing
that happens can be more terrible. I am numb when it comes to death.
I'm sorry when it happens to other people, but it feels as if someone
has just left the room and moved on never to return. Maybe that's all it
is. But my mother returns with every memory, every smell and colour,
every sound of music.

Where her picture in the forefront of my mind had been now hangs
a jagged, torn emptiness which will never be repaired. I now imagine a
gold frame round it and remember who had been there once.

The last time my sister Tessa and I saw our mother was in London
a few months before she died on 26 May 1969. She stood outside the
Royal Overseas Club where she was staying, wearing her ostrich leather
coat and a hat, looking like Ingrid Bergman. Always smart, elegant and
in control. Then she went back to Cape Town and lost control. One
morning she got into her car, drove from Pinelands, through Newlands

and past Kirstenbosch, across Constantia Neck and into Hout Bay, not stopping until she reached the highest point on Chapman's Peak. She stopped the car and left a note on top of the ostrich leather coat neatly folded. And jumped down onto the jagged rocks below. There would be no second attempt. No exit for sissies.

Suicide is suicide. Looking back now after all those years that feel like a long dark moment, I'm certain the right medication for depression and thyroid disorders would have made her life liveable. In 1969 it wasn't available. She felt she was going mad and in her worst moment of terror she went and took our lives with her.

My background as a child growing up in South Africa was both ordinary and extraordinary. My father, Hannes Uys, was an Afrikaner; my mother, Helga Bassel, German. Not ordinary, but not unusual in a country rife with international marriages. The fact that both parents were pianists was special.

The secret that my mother was Jewish was extraordinary. She died when I was in my twenties and only then did we find out that she was not just a refugee from Nazi Germany, but also a Jew. That makes me a Jewish Afrikaner. At least I can say I belong to both chosen people.

I have a small framed letter next to my desk. I'm looking at it now as I do every time I sit and write here. It is dated 19 August 1935 and addressed to Helga Bassel, Neue Kantstrasse 16, Berlin-Charlottenburg. It is from Dr Peter Raabe, President of the Reichs-Musikkammer. Although it is in official German and defies easy translation, the letter says the following:

> Because you are a member of the Jewish race, you will no longer be allowed to practise your career as a pianist. No professional venue will be allowed to employ you. You may no longer perform in Germany.

Helga Bassel did perform in Germany for the next four years, playing Mozart, Beethoven, Liszt, Scarlatti and Chopin, flaunting her art and contempt for the Nazis until 1938, when her frightened friends took her to Bremenhaven and put her on a boat which eventually docked in Cape Town.

One of her first engagements was with the Cape Town City Orchestra, playing a two-piano Mozart Concerto with a young local pianist called

Hannes Uys. I look at this letter all the time. It's just a little letter. Like so many other little letters, it is powerful enough to end a dream and cut short a life. Not unlike a familiar local sign that once said 'Whites Only'.

We never spoke politics at home, because Pa said it was a dirty thing. He was right, but unfortunately all those politicians who lead us into hell got away with the dirt still under their nails, because we didn't audition them and take charge.

We never spoke of Germany. Sometimes Helga would tell us about the snow in Berlin and the iced-up Lietzensee outside her home. The horrible things were left to Hollywood movies. When Marlene Dietrich came to Cape Town in 1966, I wanted to take my mother because surely they shared so much, both coming from Berlin. My mother didn't want to go.

Our dining room in Pinelands was more of an alcove, with two long benches against the walls with the long table between, ending in the bay window of small square panes like an Elizabethan cottage in Stratford. Tessa and I, being the smallest and the children, sat in this alcove at the end of the benches. The guests filled the rest of the space. Usually eight people, from all over the world. Musicians, painters, travellers, with many languages and accents. And Uncle Andre who was a ballet dancer and played the part offstage to perfection. His hair was edged with purple and rouge glowed on his cheeks. He knew Margot and Rudi and Gary and Phyllis and his stories were divine darling.

I was twelve, blond, and instinctively sensed power. Although no one had told me (because in those days no one spoke about those things called the facts of survival), I saw Uncle Andre's furtive looks and knew when to wag my Persian cat-tail. And so he sat beside me at the dinner table. His knee pressed against my leg. Not overtly, probably not on purpose, but then again in tribute to him, he wasn't going to let such a chance pass by. I was playing reactions in close-up for an MGM camera. A huff, a sigh, a squirm, a raised eyebrow. No one took any notice. They were discussing the recent Salzburg Music Festival.

Ma was in the kitchen preparing the Wiener Schnitzel with Sannie Abader, our maid, a woman who could now speak German with an Athlone accent and cook like a Kraut. In a huff little Pieter Uys pushed past the guests along the bench and stalked into the kitchen, ready for a showdown and a scene.

'Ma? Uncle Andre touched my leg!' he said, nearly lisping with affront.

'Well Darling, if you don't like it, sit somewhere else. Here, take in the beans.' And that was that.

That was Ma. Don't like it? Move. None of us could indulge in the luxury of being sick. Or bunking school. When we came out with that pathetic Mommy-I'm-not-feeling-well voice, she'd shrug and say: 'It'll pass. Go to school.' And it did pass. And she was right.

I wonder what we would say to each other today. I'm now a year older than she was when her life ended. She always said I would write.

She was right.

Pieter-Dirk Uys is a satirist born in Cape Town. He is known for using humour and stand-up comedy to criticise and expose the absurdity of the South African apartheid government's racial policies. He is particularly well known for his persona Evita Bezuidenhout, a white Afrikaner socialite and self-proclaimed political activist. He is also an author and works in the forefront of HIV/AIDS activism and education.

Ashwin Willemse

HOPE ITSELF

My grandmother, Maria Lewis, born
8 February 1933 in Bredasdorp;
my mother, Stawa, born Gustava
Willemse, on 14 June 1963 in Grabouw

People think of me and perhaps they remember the Springbok with the best smile of 2003; the man with the green gum guard who seemed to disappear for a long time after 2004, only to make a surprise comeback just in time to be included in the Bok team of 2007, the team that went on to win the World Cup. People may even remember that in 2003 I was Springbok of the Year, Newcomer of the Year and also, as voted by his teammates, Players' Player of the Year. That was a good year. Those who know more may even think of me as the Springbok who came from a life of gangsterism, drugs, crime and a failed teen suicide attempt. Those were not good years.

What people don't know is that I never met my father until after school. They don't know that I am the product of the love, faith and strength of two incredible women – my mother and my grandmother.

My grandmother was born Maria Lewis on 8 February 1933 in Bredasdorp and my mother, Stawa, was born Gustava Willemse on 14 June 1963 in Grabouw.

My father left my mother when she was still pregnant. He had a wife and family, unbeknown to her, in Johannesburg. The next man to come into her life was similarly untruthful and did much the same to her. That's how I got my brother Bertie. She raised us with the care of a mother, but with all the strictness of a father. In my community, in Caledon, a small town in the Western Cape not too far from Cape Town, absent fathers were a chronic affliction. Many of my cousins and friends never knew theirs.

My grandmother was tough enough to have come through many difficult years and a great deal of poverty with all her faith and her body intact. She was lucky with her husband, and she and he are still together after more than fifty years of marriage. When my mother found a good man, who lived in Eerste River, forty minutes drive away, I was thirteen, and she asked for my permission to marry him. I just wanted her to be happy. She was still a young woman looking for love, but it meant that my grandmother was tasked with raising me.

During my high-school years this became ever more difficult. Our house was full of family, few of whom worked, and I lived in a shack outside with the men. Sometimes even the family would question why I was staying there instead of with my mom, but my grandmother never once made me feel like an outsider. Even during the toughest of times she made an effort to make things special. When there wasn't enough money for bread, and all she could afford was maize meal, she would colour the maize meal with a different food colouring each day, and a different flavour of Sweeto cooldrink concentrate. I'd even place bets about what colour the pap was going to be on a particular day. It showed the marvellous, gentle, loving way she had of trying to preserve child-hood and distracting us from how abominably poor we really were.

She prayed all the time. I think there is a spot on her knees worn through just from all the prayers for Bertie and me. She gave me my faith in God. Even when I was most off the given path, selling drugs, robbing and moving up in a gang, I would spend much of my ill-gotten money on her, even going so far as to buy her several portraits of Jesus. It was hardly a redeeming act, but I think that her prayers for me finally bore fruit. Against all conceivable odds, I became a Springbok. I have been in the team for two successive World Cups, and my inclusion the second time was nothing short of a miracle.

When grandmothers pray, believe me, miracles are possible. I re-member that one of my proudest moments was when I finally played at Newlands stadium. As fate would have it, I was living in Johannesburg then, playing for the Cats in the Super Twelve. The Cats were having the most horrendous season and it didn't go any better in that game against the Stormers. I don't think of that, though. I think of seeing my mother and grandmother, standing together there in the stands, cheering me on. My aunt was with them and she told me afterwards that she'd hardly been able to follow the game because my mom and grandma had been far too excited throughout. My grandmother had just kept on shouting: 'Come on Storms!' and my mother had kept on correcting her, telling her that she was saying it wrong: 'They're the Storemans!' she'd screamed. I don't know who won their argument. They were both wrong in any case and, either way, *attempting* to cheer for the team that I wasn't actually *in*.

I think back to that day and I smile. They don't know much about rugby, but without a mother and a grandmother like mine, how many sports stars could really say that they would have been able to make it? I don't know. Certainly, it's not something I would ever dare to say. Because, when I look into my grandma's eyes, I see a glimmer there that is nothing else but the loving face of God. And it was that power, channelled through the old, wrinkled, tiny hands of a diminutive lady living in a poor coloured township that allowed me to run on the grasses of Ellis Park, Twickenham, Dunedin and Lansdowne Road, be watched by millions as I scored a try and gave a green smile. Perhaps it's all because of my grandma's diet of green pap. Maybe there was something more than just colouring and sweetener in that pap. Perhaps what was in that pap was hope itself.

Ashwin Willemse was born in Caledon in the Western Cape and is a rugby union player for the Springboks. He was one of the outstanding performers during the 2003 season, being awarded Player of the Year, Most Promising Player of the Year and Players' Player of the Year.

Acknowledgements

There have been so many who accompanied me on this journey of compiling this book:

I am so blessed to have, as my dearest circle of love, my husband Jim and my daughter Thandi, who never stop believing in me, my parents Inge and Dieter Keim and my grandmother Martha Fischer who love me across the world and gave me all the ingredients for becoming a mother. I would like to thank my dearest circle of friends Margaret Gwegwe, Elise Elsing and Nicole Brandt for the sisterhood, my friends Leonard and Elree Seelig, Odette and Clive Hubbard and Diane Flannery who never stopped encouraging me, Andre Brandt, Ian Puttkammer and Georgia Baerveldt who helped in trial and error, my colleagues Lois Dippenaar and Antjie Krog who always so enthusiastically offered their rich advice and Prof. Brian O'Connell who offered his much appreciated support.

I particularly want to thank a very special woman, Issa Seelig, who involuntarily gave birth to this book and put the spark in my heart.

I also wish to thank my publisher Umuzi who liked the idea from the start, the agencies, photographers and all the authors who made their photos available for this book. The organisations Women for Peace and Global Buddies for their very much appreciated support for the cover. See page 176 for more information.

And last but not least I am eternally grateful and remain indebted to every single author who so willingly and enthusiastically offered a glimpse into their very personal lives by sharing these wonderful and deep stories about those special women in their lives, their mothers and grandmothers, who shaped their world and ours.

MK

Publisher's note

The publisher and compiler acknowledge Muhtadia Rice and Charles Cilliers for assisting Yvonne Chaka Chaka and Ashwin Willemse respectively.

Permission to reproduce an extract from *Boyhood* by JM Coetzee is granted by Secker & Warberg.

The piece by Miriam Makeba is from the personal collection of Miriam Makeba, courtesy of the ZM Makeba Trust.

Nelson Mandela's piece is a compilation by Marion Keim and is mostly extracted from *Long Walk to Freedom* by Nelson Mandela, first published by Little Brown, 1994. Paragraph three on page 100 is taken from *Mandela: The Authorized Portrait* by Mac Maharaj, Ahmed Kathrada, et al., first published by Wild Dog Press in Association with PQ Blackwell in 2006. The indented quotation on page 105 comes from a prison notebook, in the Nelson Mandela Centre of Memory and Dialogue. Permission is provided with the much appreciated support of the Nelson Mandela Foundation.

Blog

Share the story of your own mother or grandmother with others on a blog we have established for this purpose.

Visit www.marionkeim@book.co.za or send your story directly to umamablog@gmail.com.

GLOBAL BUDDIES

Women for Peace is a community upliftment organisation based in Mfuleni, Cape Town. Through peace development, skills training and after-school programmes, the group helps women and children build better lives for themselves and their community. The partner programme for Women for Peace in the United States, **Global Buddies**, brings a group of American families to Mfuleni each year to participate in cultural exchange and community service with South African families, giving children from both countries the chance to make connections across cultural boundaries and build a sense of global citizenship.